Rod Crossfield is a former intelligence analyst and police officer. He holds commercial certificates for both airplane and helicopter and makes his living in aviation.

He is the author of the Detective Donnelly mysteries and of Remembering the Good Stuff: Memoirs From The Heartland, as well as various aviation-related works. He also writes the It Says Here commentaries.

He is currently at work on a techno-thriller novel. He divides his time between the Caribbean and America's heartland.

If you enjoy this book and would like to see more writing from Rod you can visit him at rodcrossfield.com to let him know. He will be pleased to hear from you.

If those of you who like this sort of natural cooking would like to send along your own variations on these recipes, or even recommend some new ones, Rod welcomes you to do so. He's always interested in good food.

ALSO BY ROD CROSSFIELD

Selected Adventures of
Detective Donnelly

Remembering The Good Stuff:
Memoirs From The Heartland

Looking Out The Window:
Memoirs of a Shade Tree Aviator

The Quick Guide to IFR Flight

The Hillbilly's Guide
to Nuclear Physics

It Says Here

INDIAN COOKING

THE LEGACY OF
JOEL REDHAWK

ROD CROSSFIELD

Foreword by
Chef Alexander Ray

FOREWORD

For a number of decades, everyday cooking in America has been a parade of artificially-sweetened, bleached, genetically-engineered tastelessness that no self-respecting citizen from former generations would consume.

A few years ago my long-time friend Rod Crossfield mentioned to me that he might someday compile the recipes found in the journal of his great-uncle, Joel Redhawk. I asked to examine them, which he graciously allowed. I encouraged him to begin his project, and although it was some time in forthcoming, this book is – finally -- the reward for his effort.

This volume brings to life the forgotten richness of naturally-produced foods. Even though these recipes are suited to simple, home cooking, in my restaurant I have served them to universal acclaim and not one of my guests has expressed a preference for more modern fare. You will have your favorites, but all are superb.

I am grateful to Rod for having shared them and I am sure that you will agree with me when I say that Mr. Redhawk knew whereof he spoke.

Alexander Ray

Hello!

We would like to introduce to you our great-uncle Joel Redhawk, of the Cherokee tribe. He was born in 1885. When he died he left to us a legacy that included much of his knowledge of Native-American cooking. Uncle Joe, as Mama called him, knew a lot about natural foods and medicine. These recipes are simple and use basic ingredients that can be varied in many ways.

YOU MUST READ THIS INTRODUCTORY SECTION!!

If you run into a hitch on a recipe it may be because you didn't read the intro. This information is vital throughout. These recipes are not from your usual modern-day cookbook. Some may not turn out as polished or refined as something from the fancy magazines. You will see that Uncle Joe had his own ways of saying and doing, and that trying to apply contemporary ingredients, tools or techniques could in some cases come back to haunt you. Remember, these recipes reflect the way it was done a hundred years ago, in the days of home-grown produce and wild game, before the use of preservatives and artificial flavorings, and with the less-than-precise wood fire to provide cooking heat.

THE RIGHT TOOLS – THIS IS IMPORTANT

Uncle Joe was very traditional – and practical -- in his techniques. He insisted on heavy, old-fashioned cookware. He refused to use aluminum pots or pans and his skillets and pans were always good, thick iron. Heavy, dense material distributes the heat more evenly. For baking he used earthenware pots (glass will work.)

When he says to beat or mix ingredients he was using the old hand beater we called a whisk. You can use a modern mixer; usually a lower speed works best.

He called a tablespoon a tablespoon, but a teaspoon was simply a spoon, although sometimes it was called a salt-spoon.

He used a wooden paddle for a spatula in places where any long-handled utensil could be used, such as tongs or a holed or slotted spoon.

And, of course, he used a wood-burning brick oven, and also cooked some things on top of a wood stove or over an open fire. Your modern kitchen range will work fine. To change the temperature he would raise or lower the pan or bank the fire a little; we will say to turn the heat up or down. Wood does add flavor, though, if you have the facilities for it.

INGREDIENTS – THIS IS EVEN MORE IMPORTANT!!

Uncle Joe always used fresh ingredients where today we might use canned or frozen. (Of course, fresh was more readily available a hundred years ago.)

Always use corn right off the cob, rather than canned or frozen.

Always use fresh tomatoes, rather than canned.

Always use fresh squash.

Always leave the peels on potatoes. That is where the flavor is. And a lot of the nutrients, too.

Never use canned beans that have already been cooked.

Never use frozen fruit. Uncle Joe grew (or knew where to get) strawberries, blackberries, mulberries, plums, peaches, grapes and apples. The store-bought fruit isn't as good nowadays, but at least get it as fresh as possible. Also, in the hills we have a wild grape called muscadine; it is very sweet. If you know someone who can get them they are much better than store-bought.

When Uncle Joe refers to onions, he means wild onions that look like what are generally called 'green onions,' the ones with the small bulbs. The wild onions are not always easy to get, and places where they grow are kept secret, but if you know someone who has them in a garden, they are the best. They are richer than regular grocery-store green onions, but those will do. If he means round white or red or yellow onions, then those are specified.

NOTE: When he calls for garlic, he means the giant-sized mild garlic we call elephant garlic. It is widely grown and commonly available. This is huge garlic, and one clove is as big as at least a half-dozen small white ones, although the white garlic has a stronger taste. The elephant kind is smoother-tasting. When he says 'clove' he means the giant clove, much bigger than the little white cloves.

There are many spices available now that Uncle Joe did not have access to, or even know about. He did use ginger and cinnamon. I believe he grew ginger, and cinnamon could be found at the store. A couple that are available nowadays that Mama used a lot are cloves and nutmeg; those were not specifically named in Uncle Joe's recipes but he supposedly used them when he could get them.

He grew what he called 'hot peppers;' what we call cayenne peppers.

He ground his own black and red pepper from peppercorns, and that is better, but store-bought ground pepper will work fine; best if it's been stored sealed from moisture.

He never used bleached flour or any bread, biscuits or muffins that were made with bleached flour. Always use unbleached. You can always simply use whole-wheat flour.

He refused to use processed sugar. He liked to use maple syrup, which he loved. He had his own stash of sugar maples somewhere in the hills, but I never met anyone who knew where they were. If you buy maple syrup be sure to get pure. Most store-bought maple syrup has sugar or corn syrup (or both) added to it, but you can find the pure stuff. READ THE LABEL! Pure maple syrup is more maple than just sweet – it makes a difference. Depending on the recipe, he occasionally used molasses, but more often plain old honey. It is important to use honey that has been produced in your area, from local plants that you are used to being around. Honey from far-away places, made from unfamiliar plants, can make your allergies act up. Uncle Joe used wild honey from bee trees he knew about in the forest.

He was very fond of raisins and used them to sweeten foods. When you don't normally eat a lot of processed sugar you develop an appreciation for how sweet natural foods really are; particularly fruits and whole grains.

Surprisingly, Uncle Joe never used lard or other animal fat; he liked to cook with vegetable oils. Sometimes he used nut oil. The most plentiful nuts around were pecans, found in the creek-bottom land. He often used pecan oil which is pressed from the nuts, but nowadays it is easier to get walnut oil or hazelnut oil at the store, and either will do. When deep-frying he would use peanut oil if it were available, because it could be made very hot without burning; he used corn oil for general purposes.

He also used pecans for recipes that called for any kind of nuts. They were the most common, and, at least to me, the best tasting.

When he calls for mushrooms he means wild ones. He knew enough about wild mushrooms to always gather all he wanted, but that is not very practical for the average cook, so you can use store-bought mushrooms – try to get them as fresh as possible. Button mushrooms, which have a smooth flavor, and portabella mushrooms, which have a rich, meaty flavor, are good for beef, venison and other red meats. Oyster mushrooms are good with poultry or pork chops.

He grew big, gourd-type squash. Nowadays two kinds that are good and sweet are butternut and buttercup. Easy to find at the store.

I don't know if he knew what margarine is, but I'm pretty sure he would have refused to use it – always use real butter. Sometimes unsalted butter will be specified. If you don't have that you need to cut down on the salt you add.

He always used fresh meat, but then, he didn't have a freezer. In any case I bet that he wouldn't have used frozen meat, but if you decide to….use your own judgment. I personally have had some pretty good meat that had been thawed.

When he refers to catfish, any catfish can be used, but his favorite (and mine) was spoonbill.

When buttermilk is called for, don't substitute regular whole milk (what we've always called 'sweet' milk.) Buttermilk adds something that sweet milk cannot, and is worth the extra trouble to obtain. Buttermilk is thought of as soured milk, but this is not accurate. It is not simply soured milk any more than cheese is soured milk. Buttermilk is its own thing, in a class by itself.

THE RECIPES

Here are a bunch of our favorite recipes from Uncle Joe, pretty much as they were dictated to his sister-in-law, my grandmother Loutisha. Some of them may not have glamorous or festive names, but Uncle Joe was very practical and called them the way he saw them. We have corrected spelling but not grammar. Each recipe and each section of similar recipes will have our own introduction.

NOTE: Some terms or phrases in the recipes may appear in parentheses; these are our clarifications or modernizations of the original instructions.

NOTE: You must read every part of the recipe! In places we have to explain what Uncle Joe meant. And, you should have read each section's introduction, too.

NOTE: You must read each recipe all the way through BEFORE you start on it!!!

See note above - Before you start on each section make sure you have read the introductory section at the beginning of the cookbook!

Most diets, in any culture in the world, start with breads. Meat is not always available, and fruits and vegetables are seasonal and may be limited in the quantities that can be raised. Breads, on the other hand, can be made from about anything you can come up with, using ingredients that can be preserved for long periods, and bread itself can be preserved in one way or another, so any culture's diet will certainly include bread.

Here are some of Uncle Joe's best bread dishes, with our own introductions to each one, and our own comments and clarifications in parentheses:

1.) FRYBREAD
2.) FRITTERS
3.) SQUASH BREAD
4.) CORNBREAD
5.) PUMPKIN FRYBREAD
6.) HO-CAKES
7.) BREAD ROLLS
8.) PUMPKIN RAISIN NUT CORNBREAD

1.) FRYBREAD

When you mention Indian bread, most people think of frybread. This is bread that is deep-fried in oil. This bread is good anytime, with anything. Fresh hot it is good with butter. As a matter of fact, it's pretty good cold with butter. It is dandy with barbequed brisket on it, or melted cheese. Or jam, or jelly, or peanut butter.

Remember, when he calls for light oil he means flower or nut oil that can be heated very hot without burning. Flour must be unbleached. And "spoon" means a teaspoon.

Uncle Joe's recipe:

1 table spoon bake powder
1 half (tea)spoon salt
3 cups (unbleached) flour
2 cups milk (you may not need all of it)
Light oil
Good heavy deep pan

Sift flour good. Warm up milk but not hot. Mix flour, milk, bake powder and salt in big bowl. Mix up. (Blend thoroughly – he used a hand whisk.) May not need all milk if on a wet day. (He means it may not take all of the milk to make it moist enough.) Make smooth, no lumps or dry places. Batter sticky put in little milk. Don't mix too hard (or dough will be tough.) Put little bit oil over top of dough and cover up. Let oil spread in. (He means let the dough rest. This will probably take half an hour or more. Cover with a damp cloth when you do this.) When dough is ready heat oil good in deep pan, little boil. (He means a low boil.) Keep oil good and hot! Quick fry makes crispy bread. Handful of dough make pancake size. (Remember to coat your hands with flour so the dough won't stick.) Let pancake into oil. Careful not to splash. Start to brown, turn over with paddle (or spatula, or tongs) fry other side. When crispy put out to drain. Good hot. Put honey or syrup (he means maple syrup.) Makes plenty. (This comes out to be quite a bit; if you're eating them with something else, like a meat dish or potatoes and eggs there will be enough for a whole table full of people.)

2.) FRITTERS

Also known as hushpuppies, these are another good fried bread, based on cornmeal; essentially deep-fried cornbread. Generally thought of as for breakfast, but good anytime. Once again a light oil is best. Best eaten when fresh and hot. "Spoon" means teaspoon.

Uncle Joe's recipe:

1 (tea)spoon bake soda
2 (tea)spoons bake powder
1 (tea)spoon salt
1 and half cups corn meal
1 half cup (unbleached) flour
1 cup buttermilk
2 eggs
Handful (wild or green) onions (enough to make a half cup chopped up)
Light oil
Good heavy deep pan

Sift cornmeal good and fine. Sift flour. Chop up onions little bits. Beat eggs. Mix cornmeal, flour, bake powder, bake soda and salt in big bowl. Put in 2 table spoons oil. Put in eggs, buttermilk and onion. Mix up good with beater. (He meant a whisk. A mixer will work fine.) Heat up oil good. Table spoon of batter into oil. Careful not to splash. When fritters rise to top of oil turn over. Wait that much time again and lift out. Drain. Eat right away, still hot enough to melt butter. Makes plenty. ('Plenty' for Uncle Joe was enough for everyone at the table to eat too much.)

3.) SQUASH BREAD

Squash has always been an important food ingredient for the Indians. Squash grows just about anywhere and will keep. There are many different kinds of squash. There are plenty of good kinds of squash at the store, but the best is either butternut or buttercup. Mama called either one butter-squash. Grated orange peel is the very thin outermost skin of the orange. Fine-grated it is called 'zest.' Don't get any of the whiter, inner peel – that part is bitter. Make it with a fine-holed grater. Honey or maple syrup, either one, can be used – they will each give a different flavor. Honey is smoother, and bakes in a little better. Maple syrup will give a sharper, richer flavor. Whichever you like. "Spoon" means teaspoon.

Uncle Joe's recipe:

2 (tea)spoons bake powder
1 half (tea)spoon bake soda
1 half (tea)spoon salt
2 cups (unbleached) flour
1 quarter cup cornmeal
1 quarter cup syrup (he means pure maple syrup)
2 big eggs
1 middle size squash (enough to make 1 cup chopped up)
1 cup raisins
Handful pecans (just the meat – enough to make ½ cup chopped up)
1 half cup oil (corn oil is fine)
Little bit orange peel (fine-grated outer colored part – see note above)
1 half (tea)spoon cinnamon (powder)
Bread pan (earthenware, ceramic or glass)

Heat oven good. (Uncle Joe used a brick oven. I don't know how he knew how hot to get it, but in a modern oven go for 325 degrees or so.) Beat eggs good. Warm up syrup (or honey) warm to pour. Mix eggs, oil and syrup. Beat good. Put in bake powder, bake soda, salt, cornmeal, flour and cinnamon (powder.) Beat good (blend thoroughly.) Chop (or grate) squash. Drain juice. Chop up pecans. Put in squash, raisins, pecans and orange peel. Make sure everything mixed real good. Batter too dry put in little bit warm milk but careful, not too much. Butter pan (grease bread pan with butter.) Put batter. Bake light-brown. (We would call it golden-brown.) Check with knife. (You want the knife to come out clean.) Good hot and good cold on next day. (This bread keeps well, if it hasn't been all eaten the first day, but usually it has.)

4.) CORNBREAD

Cornbread is always good, with just about anything you eat. Good with beans, soup, stew, you name it. This is classic cornbread. Cook fresh corn and cut the kernels off the cobs. Lightly roast the corn ahead of time for more flavor. Use a heavy iron pan.

Uncle Joe's recipe:

1 and half (tea)spoons bake powder
1 half (tea)spoon salt
1 table spoon honey
2 table spoons oil
1 half cup cornmeal
3 quarters cup (unbleached) flour
1 half cup (whole kernel) corn (use fresh!)
1 half cup buttermilk
3 eggs
1 little tomato (chop up enough to make a half cup)
Little handful (wild or green) onions (chop up enough to make 1 half cup)
Little bit garlic (Uncle Joe used the big mild elephant garlic. The bulb is big as a grapefruit; use a small part of a clove, about one quarter, to season.)
Good heavy pan (glass is fine)

Heat oven good. (Here we are again. How did he know how hot his old brick oven was? Set your modern oven good and hot, 400 degrees or so.) Roast corn little bit. (Don't let it get tough.) Put pan in oven to get hot too. Beat up eggs real good. Put in big bowl. Chop up garlic, onions and tomato. Put in big bowl. Warm up honey to pour. Put in big bowl. Put in corn, buttermilk, cornmeal, flour, oil, salt and bake powder. Mix up good (blend thoroughly.) Make batter good and smooth. Butter pan good (grease with butter.) Put in batter. Bake. Check center with knife. (Knife should come out clean – this should take 20 minutes or so.) Let cool little bit, still warm. (I have been known to eat half a pan of this myself; till it gets cool enough to quit melting the butter.)

NOTE: Mama sometimes added a teaspoon of ground sage, which is a sausage seasoning, to the batter.

5.) PUMPKIN FRYBREAD

Another frybread. This one is sweet and spicy, using the ever-popular pumpkin. Good with jam. Also very good with chicken or turkey, or duck or goose, for that matter. When you slaughter the pumpkin save the seeds; we will roast them later for snacks. "Spoon" means teaspoon.

Uncle Joe's recipe:

2 (tea)spoons bake powder
1 half (tea)spoon salt
1 quarter (tea)spoon cinnamon (powder)
3 cups (unbleached) flour
1 cup pumpkin (the meat, chopped to make one cup)
1 half cup syrup (pure maple syrup – no sugar added)
1 and half cups milk (you may not need all of it)
Light oil (peanut oil is good)
Good heavy (iron) pan

Sift flour good. Put flour, bake powder, cinnamon and salt in big bowl. Put in (chopped) pumpkin. Stir up good. Warm up (maple) syrup to pour. Put in. Put in half table spoon oil. Stir up good. Warm up milk but not hot. May not need all milk (depends on the humidity) don't make too thin. Mix up good. Make smooth, no lumps or dry places. Batter sticky put in little more milk. Don't mix too hard (or the dough will be tough.) Put little bit oil over top of dough and cover. Let oil spread in. (He means spread oil over the top and let the dough rest. This will probably take half an hour or more. Use a damp cloth to cover with.) When dough is ready heat oil in pan, little boil. (He means a low boil.) Keep oil good and hot. Quick fry makes light bread. Take little handful dough and make ball (golf ball-sized.) Put flour on hands! (so the dough won't stick.) Don't squeeze too hard or bread will be heavy. (You don't want the dough compressed so much that the bread is dense.) Let dough ball into oil. Careful not to splash. Don't let balls stick together. Little bit turn over with paddle (or spatula, or tongs) fry other side. Don't cook too long. (Golden brown.) Put out to drain. Put syrup. (He means on top. This makes a big bowl full of small roll-size breads.)

6.) HO-CAKES

These are corn pancakes. Mama made them by the bushel, and we ate them quick as she pulled them off the griddle. I would stand by the stove and butter and eat one while I was waiting for the next one to get done. She used honey, but Uncle Joe preferred maple syrup. Your choice.

Uncle Joe's recipe:

1 half (tea)spoon salt
1 cup fine cornmeal
2 table spoons syrup (<u>pure</u> maple syrup)
1 and a half cups cream (or milk – cream is better)
Light oil

Heat up griddle good and hot. (You can use a good, heavy iron skillet.) Heat cream warm but not hot. Warm up syrup to pour. Mix cornmeal, syrup, cream and salt. Make smooth, no lumps or dry places. May not need all cream – don't make too thin. Butter up griddle (grease with butter.) Fry both sides. (This will take longer than regular flour-type pancakes, several minutes. You will have to experiment to get the timing down. Cakes should be crispy at the edges and grainy inside.) Eat hot. (We did.)

7.) BREAD ROLLS

These are light breads, like dinner rolls, but deep fried. You fry them quickly, so that they don't get hard. Use them anywhere you'd use regular dinner rolls. Very simple.

Uncle Joe's recipe:

2 table spoons bake powder

1 half (tea)spoon salt

2 cups (unbleached) flour

1 cup milk

Few (wild or green) onions (chop up enough to make a quarter cup)

1 half (tea)spoon cinnamon (powder) (this is optional)

2 (tea)spoons syrup (he means maple syrup, however, honey works better for dinner rolls)

Light oil

Good heavy (iron) fry pan (doesn't need to be deep.)

Warm up syrup to pour. Warm up milk, not hot. Chop up onions little bitty pieces. Put in bowl. Put in flour, salt and bake powder (and cinnamon.) Stir up good. Put in syrup and milk. Mix up good (blend thoroughly; make the batter smooth.) Heat up pan full of oil good and hot to little boil. (He means low boil, almost bubbling.) Quick fry makes light rolls. Table spoon batter in oil. Careful not to splash. Turn over, make both sides light brown. (We would call it golden-brown.) Put out to drain. Good with meat. (They are.)

8.) PUMPKIN RAISIN NUT CORNBREAD

More pumpkin goodies. This is a sweet rich cornbread, good to use instead of dressing. Lots of different ways to spice it up; you can even use red pepper or jalapenos to make it hot, if you like. The zest is fine-grated lemon peel -- the very thin outermost skin of the lemon. Don't get any of the whiter, inner peel – that part is bitter. Make it with a fine-holed grater.

Uncle Joe's recipe:

1 (tea)spoon bake powder
1 half (tea)spoon salt
1 cup cornmeal
1 cup (unbleached) flour
2 eggs
1 and half cups pumpkin (enough of the meat chopped to make a cup and a half)
Handful pecans (just the meat -- enough to make a half cup chopped)
1 half cup raisins
1 half cup milk (or buttermilk)
1 half cup syrup (pure maple syrup or honey – we always used honey)
1 half cup butter (you can use oil)
1 (tea)spoon cinnamon (powder)
(We add:
   1 teaspoon lemon 'zest' [see intro] - optional
   1 quarter teaspoon ground ginger – optional)
Good heavy bread pan (Glass will work. He used iron or earthenware)

Heat up oven good. (Here we go again – how did he know how hot his brick oven was? Set your oven for baking, 350 degrees.) Chop up pecans. Cook (bake) pumpkin meat and mash fine. (It can be pureed in the blender.) Warm up syrup (or honey) to pour. Melt butter. Beat eggs. Mix up eggs, milk, syrup, butter, pumpkin, nuts and raisins. Mix good. Put in flour, cornmeal, salt, cinnamon (powder) and bake powder (and ginger and lemon zest, if you like.) Mix up but not too hard. Mix too much will make batter tough. (Mama liked to add the wet to the dry; in any case mix gently and thoroughly.) Butter pan good (grease with butter.) Put batter (in pan.) Bake light-brown. (Remember we want golden-brown.) Check with knife. (You want the knife to come out clean.) Good hot. (Also good cold the next day.)

Before you start on each section make sure you have read the introductory section at the beginning of the cookbook!

The old-timers used whatever meat was available, whether it was beef, pork, poultry, fish or wild game. Various of these recipes work for venison, small game such as rabbit or squirrel, panfish, catfish, turkey, duck, quail and goose. It's all good. Snake meat is actually quite good, but stay away from possum. And the old grocery-store trio of cow/pig/chicken will work just fine. You will see that some recipes refer simply to 'meat,' rather than specifically steak, or venison, or chicken, or rabbit, or whatever. Those recipes will work for most any meat; but remember, in the old days you cooked what you could get, and it might be different every week. Check each recipe's notes for variations in ingredients for red meats versus white meats.

With our own intros and our comments/clarifications in parentheses:

1.) MEAT PIES
2.) BIG-GAME FRY STEW
3.) CORNMEAL BATTER CATFISH
4.) GRIDDLE-FRY CHICKEN with NUTS & MUSHROOMS
5.) CHILI
6.) HOT-FRY CATFISH
7.) PEMMICAN
8.) SMOKED JERKY
9.) MEAT SOUP
10.) SAUSAGE MUFFINS
11.) PECAN CHOPPED ROAST
12.) FISH CAKES
13.) MUSHROOM BURGERS
14.) SMALL-GAME FRY STEW
15.) SMOKED MEAT SPREAD
16.) GRILLED MEAT with SWEET SAUCE
17.) CHICKEN POTATO SOUP
18.) GRILLED MEAT with MUSHROOM SAUCE

1.) MEAT PIES

These are the old classic handy meal. Sort of like the modern "Hot Pockets." You can put about anything you like in them, from taco-filling to pizza ingredients, or fruit, or chocolate cream. However, for now we'll start with Uncle Joe's old-faithful basic handy snacks. Don't roast the pecans too long or they'll get tough. First, the meat filling.

Uncle Joe's recipe:

1 pound meat (your choice – beef, pork, chicken, rabbit, you name it)
1 half cup raisins
Handful pecans (just the meat – enough to make ½ cup chopped)
Light oil (he means peanut oil or similar)
Little handful onions (dozen or so wild or green onions)
1 (tea)spoon (ground) sage
1 (tea)spoon pepper (ground black pepper)
1 hot pepper (he means a cayenne pepper; you can use a chili pepper or whatever you like)

Already roast pecans. (Roast the chopped pecan-meat in the oven, not too long.) Chop up meat (beef or whatever. Make it like chopped brisket.) Chop up onion and (hot) pepper good. Pan on good hot fire. (Use a good, heavy iron skillet.) Quick fry (sear) meat in oil. Keep frying. Put in onions and (hot) pepper. Stir good. Put in black pepper and sage. Stir up. Medium fire (turn down.) Put in raisins and pecans. Mix up good. Slow cook (he means simmer for a few minutes.) Drain. (This is a good time to put in barbeque sauce if you like.) Put in (inside the) bread pies. (Now for the pastry. This is a cornbread pie-shell.)

1 half cup cornmeal
1 and half cups (unbleached) flour
1 half cup milk
2 table spoons corn oil
1 (tea)spoon salt
Light oil for pot

Warm up milk not hot. Sift cornmeal good and fine. Put cornmeal, flour, and salt in bowl. Put in (corn) oil and milk. Mix up good to make dough. Don't mix too hard (or the dough will be tough.) Let sit. (He means let the dough rest, about half hour. Be sure to cover it.) Roll out dough big as your hand. (Palm-sized; make a four-inch circle of dough with the rolling pin.) Put meat filling on flat dough. (A heaping tablespoon.) Bend over and mash (edges) together (make half circle shapes.) Heat up oil in pot, good and hot. Fry hot to cook quick. (The hotter the oil the crisper and lighter the pie. Use an iron pot or deep iron skillet.) Pies in hot oil. Careful not to splash! Turn over. Make sure light brown both sides (he means golden-brown.) Put out to drain. (These are good even without anything to go with them, but fried potatoes are a good side dish.)

2.) BIG-GAME FRY STEW

This is a tasty stew that uses skillet browned meat instead of roast. Good way to prepare venison, but beef works fine. Or pork. The potatoes to use are the small, red-skinned ones that are so good in stew. Regular garlic will work but we have always used the elephant garlic which is milder and sweeter. Uncle Joe used wild mushrooms, but the store-bought kind will work. Use portabella mushrooms for red meat, or if you make this with pork use oyster mushrooms. When he calls for 'stock' you can use meat broth. You can brew a handful of bouillon cubes in a cup of water to get a beef stock that will work, but that will be salty so you'd need to be careful adding salt later. Use chicken bouillon for pork, and brew it with milk instead of water. This stew is a basic dish, so you can vary the seasoning as you prefer.

Uncle Joe's recipe:

2 pounds meat (anything!)
Double handful stew potatoes (2 pounds)
Big handful (wild or green) onions (couple dozen)
Big handful mushrooms (we will chop them up to make 1 cup– see note above for best type)
1 big tomato
1 bunch carrots (half pound)
2 big stalks celery
1 clove garlic (he means the elephant garlic – these are BIG cloves)
Stock (broth or bouillon)
1 half cup oil
1 (tea)spoon black pepper
1 half (tea)spoon (ground) sage
1 quarter (tea)spoon salt

Cut up meat in stew pieces. Cut up potatoes, celery, carrots and mushrooms and tomato. Chop up onions and garlic little bitty pieces. Heat up oil in stew pot good and hot. (This can be a deep iron skillet.) Brown meat in pot. (Sear the meat to hold in the juices.) Drain (oil) good. Medium fire (turn down) to bake. Put in all other things. Cover with stock. Stir up good. Cover pot. Cook (till) potatoes are done. (You can add other spices. Mama liked to put in a couple of mint leaves. Daddy like to put in Louisiana Hot Sauce, which has vinegar in it. Any way you make it, this stew is really good with cornbread on the side.

3.) CORNMEAL BATTER CATFISH

As I mentioned, our favorite catfish is spoonbill, but you can't always get those. They are found most often in the big rivers. You can always use regular old pond catfish, or channel cats – all good. The beer used in the recipe gives a rich flavor from the malt and such, and the alcohol cooks away. Use a good heavy beer, not a light one.

Uncle Joe's recipe:

3 pounds catfish
1 cup cornmeal
1 half cup (unbleached) flour
1 cup buttermilk
1 half can beer (this would be 6 ounces)
2 big eggs (Mama always used jumbo size – that's what our hens laid)
Little handful (wild or green) onions (about a dozen or so)
1 (tea)spoon black pepper
1 (tea)spoon salt
(Optional: you can also add ½ teaspoon of cayenne, ginger, cinnamon, chili powder, lemon juice or other preferred seasoning if you like. Mama liked ginger and lemon. Daddy liked chili powder.)
Oil (Corn oil will do fine, since it doesn't need to be really, really hot.)
2 (mixing) bowls
(Iron pot or deep frying pan)

Heat up oil in pot over fire, not too hot. (You don't need to fry as hot as you do breads.) Cut up fish. (1 inch cubes are about right.) Chop up onions little. Beat eggs. Put eggs, buttermilk, onions and beer in one bowl. Mix up. (Don't stir too hard or the beer will foam!) Sift cornmeal good and fine. Put cornmeal, flour, black pepper and salt (and any other seasonings you like) in other bowl. Dip fish pieces in wet (buttermilk and egg) bowl. Roll in dry (cornmeal) bowl. Put pieces in hot oil. Fry (till) crusty. Don't cook too long. (If you leave them in too long the meat will get brown and tough.) Dip out with paddle (or spatula, or tongs, or spoon.) Put out to drain. (Channel cat cubes are good with a dab of butter on them; spoonbill is so rich you probably won't need the butter. Spoonbill is the lobster of fresh-water fish.)

4.) GRIDDLE-FRY CHICKEN WITH NUTS & MUSHROOMS

This is a good way to fix chicken breast meat. It is battered and seared in a skillet with mushrooms and seasoned with onions and spices and pecans. It is very tasty. Uncle Joe used only wild mushrooms, but if you don't have a source for those you can use grocery-store mushrooms. Wild or not, my favorite with chicken are oyster mushrooms. We generally like red pepper, rather than black, with chicken. Be sure to read the notes about not getting the fire too hot. Don't roast the pecan meats too long or they'll get tough.

Uncle Joe's recipe:

1 and half pounds chicken (not counting bones)

Big handful pecans (just the meat – enough to make 1 cup chopped)

Big handful mushrooms (we will chop them up to make 1 cup – see note above for best type)

Little handful (wild or green) onions (about a dozen)

1 cup cornmeal

1 half cup chicken stock (you can use chicken bouillon)

1 half (tea)spoon pepper (fine red or black)

1 half (tea)spoon ginger

(Here is a good place, also, for a half teaspoon of your favorite spice such as basil, or even chili powder if you like that with chicken)

1 half (tea)spoon (or less – your taste – remember the bouillon is salty) salt

Oil for frying (corn oil will work but nut oil tastes better)

Already roast pecans. (Just the meat, not too long.) Chop up (in) little bitty pieces. Heat up oil medium in skillet over fire. (If you fry the meat too hot it will darken and get tough.) Sift cornmeal good and fine. Chop up mushrooms. Chop up onions. Put cornmeal, (red) pepper, ginger and salt (and whatever else you like with chicken) in bowl. Mix up good. Cut chicken fry pieces. (You can leave the breasts whole, but they will cook more evenly if you cut into little flat slabs.) Roll chicken pieces in powder. Fry in skillet. (Here what he means is to sear the chicken as bit before you cook it with the other ingredients. This is essentially sauté – be sure and shake the skillet so that the meat doesn't stick and get overcooked spots.) Medium fire (turn down.) Put in onions, mushrooms and (chicken) stock. Cover up and cook slow. (Simmer for a few minutes.) Drain. Spread on (garnish with) pecans. (If you haven't over-cooked the chicken it will cut with a fork.)

5.) CHILI

We make this by the big pot full. We always had this on holidays when we watched the football games. You can use regular garlic but we have always used elephant garlic, which is smoother and sweeter – not as strong. The bulb is as big as a grapefruit. When Uncle Joe specifies a clove of garlic he means an elephant clove; one of them would make a regular garlic bulb. If you use regular garlic you don't need as much because it's stronger. He grew chili peppers; store-bought will be fine. Garden tomatoes are best if you can get them; the ones at the store don't have much flavor nowadays. Yellow onions are best for this. He used cayenne peppers, but we've always used jalapenos. If you have a pepper grinder fresh-ground black and red pepper is better; otherwise buy fine-ground. Usually you use beef or venison, but chicken or turkey make good chili, and so do pork chops. We double or triple the ingredients to make more, but this is a good place to start. Remember, use heavy iron cookware if possible.

Uncle Joe's recipe:

2 pounds meat (stew meat)
1 pound beans (he means pinto beans – this is optional)
1 pound corn (whole kernel corn)
2 big yellow onions
1 big tomato (or small ones, you'll need about 2 cups chopped)
1 clove garlic (remember, the big elephant garlic clove)
Big handful green chili (he means the peppers – 2 to 3 cups chopped)
1 big or 2 little hot chili pepper (You can use more if you like hotter.)
2 cups stock (beef broth – you can use bouillon)
1 (tea)spoon red (cayenne) pepper
1 (tea)spoon black pepper
(Optional: Mama would sometimes add a bay leaf or two; up to you. Use bay leaves as fresh as possible.)
Salt (to taste)
Oil (corn oil is good)

Cook beans in stock good and slow (all morning.) Slow-roast corn. (NOTE: This is good, but you can just boil the corn and then sear it when you sauté the other ingredients. If you roast, use low heat. Be careful not to over cook, or the corn will get tough.) Chop up meat. (We make it fine like brisket to bring out the flavor.) Chop up onions. Chop up tomato medium size. Chop up green chili (peppers) fine. Chop up hot chili pepper fine. Chop up garlic. Grind up (red and black) pepper. Heat up oil in pan good and hot. Quick fry (he means sauté for a minute) meat, onions, (corn, if you use boiled corn,) garlic and hot peppers. Keep stirred. (Shake pan or ingredients will stick and get burned spots.) Pour off oil. Put (meat, etc.) in pot. Low fire. Put beans (optional,) tomato, green chilis, red and black pepper and salt. Put in stock (from beans.) Cover. Slow cook (simmer for 1 hour on low heat.) Good on bread. (This is good in a bowl with crackers, corn chips, biscuits, or my favorite, hunks of longhorn cheese.)

6.) HOT-FRY CATFISH

Uncle Joe didn't call it sauté; he called it hot-fry, or quick-fry, but it is oil-frying fish without using batter coating. Another case of not getting the skillet too hot. Fish will darken and toughen if it is too hot, and burns easily. It is important to shake the skillet or stir the fish and turn it in a timely manner. This is where you use what he called 'light' oil, peanut or similar. Fish is better with a lighter oil than with corn oil. (For that matter so is chicken.) This also is where the smoother elephant garlic shines. Catfish is best this way, and spoonbill is the best catfish, but you can cook perch or crappie filets this way too. In that case you might add a teaspoon of lemon juice, or serve it on the side.

Uncle Joe's recipe:

3 pounds catfish (he means 3 lb filet)
Little handful (wild or green) onions (about a dozen)
1 clove garlic (the big elephant garlic – that would be half a dozen regular cloves)
(Optional: ¼ teaspoon ginger or cinnamon)
1 half stick (unsalted) butter
Pinch salt
Light oil

Cut up catfish in flat bite-chunks. (These are pieces about 1-1/2 by 2-1/2 inches and ½ inch thick. They look like little pork chops.) Chop up onion and garlic good and fine. Melt butter. Put enough oil in pan to cover bottom good. Heat up medium hot over fire. (Remember, not too hot.) Put in butter, onions, garlic and salt. Stir up good. (If you want to add ginger or cinnamon or something else do it now.) Put in fish. Hot-fry both sides. (This will take a few minutes. If the heat is right you will get a bit of golden-brown tinge to each side and the slightest suggestion of crispiness at the edges.) Eat hot. (These are really good with those brown-and-serve dinner rolls.)

7.) PEMMICAN

Pemmican is a generic term usually meaning some combination of meat, bread, berries and nuts compressed into cakes or blocks. Uncle Joe had a word for it which more-or-less meant 'journey-cakes,' as it was used as a carry-along food for traveling or for hunting trips. Beef jerky and the modern trail-mixes are the more familiar forms nowadays. You can use our jerky recipe, which follows this one, or your favorite brand of store-bought jerky. In his oatmeal recipes he used rolled oats, but it is simpler to use old-fashioned uncooked oatmeal.

Uncle Joe's recipe:

2 pounds jerky
Big handful pecans (just the meat – enough to make one cup chopped)
1 cup raisins
1 cup oats (uncooked – just use old-fashioned oatmeal)
1 half cup oil

Heat oven medium hot. (Baking heat – about 350 degrees. He used a brick oven, and no thermometer, but he could always get it right.) Chop up jerky fine. Chop up pecans. Put jerky, pecans, raisins, oats and oil in big bowl. Mix up real good. Mash together hard. Make cakes. (Snack-sized cakes about as big as a hamburger patty.) Butter pan (grease with butter) to put cakes. Bake in oven, not too long. (You don't want them crispy-done like cookies, but chewy-done.) Good to take along. (A variation is to use cornmeal instead of oats and make them corn pemmican instead of oat pemmican.)

8.) SMOKED JERKY

Smoked jerky is simple to make, and you can use any kind of meat. Uncle Joe used his wood-burning brick oven, and when he wanted to smoke something he simply burned hickory wood and got the good smoke flavor. You can use a table-top smoker, which can be bought reasonably at any big sporting-goods store, feed-store, ranch supply or discount warehouse like Wal-Mart or Target. Use damp wood chips to get the smoke. DON'T use old pine boards unless you want the jerky to taste like turpentine; use chips of hardwood such as hickory or mesquite. You can get them by the bag at the same places that sell smokers.

Jerky will keep indefinitely, I hear, although we always eat it all up the first day. A marvelous low-calorie, low-fat snack that is pretty much addictive. It can be seasoned a jillion different ways. You can use beef, venison, turkey, pork, chicken, rabbit, you name it. (In the old days buffalo was used a lot, but that's not as easy to get as it once was.) Start with whatever is handy.

Uncle Joe's recipe:

4 pounds meat
1 quarter cup salt
1 (tea)spoon black pepper
1 (tea)spoon garlic powder
1 (tea)spoon ginger powder (ground ginger)
1 half (tea)spoon cinnamon (powder)
1 quarter cup maple sugar (brown sugar will work, if necessary, but don't use white
sugar.)

Heat oven (or smoker) low heat. (This is not hot by cooking standards, about 150 degrees.) Cut up meat. Make hand-size strips (6 inches long if the meat's that big, and about an inch wide.) Make thin. (Cut them as thin as you can, no more than about 1/4 inch. You need a good, sharp knife!) Put black pepper, garlic powder, ginger, (maple) sugar, cinnamon and salt in pan. Mix up good. Roll meat pieces in pan. (Coat with powders.) Put in oven (or smoker) all day. (When the jerky is done enough you can break a piece in your hand. You don't want it brittle, make it chewy. You can use your kitchen oven the same way, you just won't have the smoke. You can always brush on a little 'liquid smoke' from a bottle before putting in the oven. Even without the smoke, though, it's pretty good.)

9.) MEAT SOUP

This is a good hearty soup that you eat with a big spoon. Very good with cornbread. No mystery about it, it is pretty basic. Use just about any cut of beef, or venison works good, too. Roasting the garlic, peppers and corn before you chop them will bring out more of their flavors. This stew is pretty hot, so you might prefer not so much pepper action.

Uncle Joe's recipe:

2 pounds meat
2 cups brown beans (we usually use pinto beans but any kind is good)
1 cup (whole kernel) corn
1 big white onion
2 big tomatoes
1 clove garlic (the big elephant-garlic)
1 (tea)spoon red (cayenne) pepper
1 (tea)spoon black pepper
Handful hot peppers (we use jalapenos)
Beef stock (bouillon will work here, but remember it is salty)
1 (tea)spoon salt (less if you use bouillon)
Oil
1 pot and 1 pan

Already roast corn, garlic and hot peppers in oven. (Watch the time – too long and they'll get tough and leathery.) Chop up onion. Cut up tomatoes stew pieces. (He means small enough that a random spoonful will have one or two pieces in it.) Put beans and tomatoes in pot. Put in (enough) stock to cover. Put on lid. Slow cook over low fire. (He means to simmer. Slower is better.) Remember to stir. (This will take a while to fully cook the beans.) Chop up meat little pieces. Chop up garlic and hot peppers. Heat oil in pan hot. Put in meat, corn, onions, garlic and hot peppers to quick fry. (Here he means to sear the meat quickly.) Medium fire (turn down) and let cook. When beans are cooked good put meat, corn, onions, garlic and hot peppers in bean pot. Put in red and black pepper and salt. Stir good. Low fire (turn down.) Slow cook (20 minutes.) Don't boil! (He means simmer.) Makes good soup. (It is good. My favorite with it is cornbread, but rolls will work, or frybread, or biscuits, or crescent rolls, or crackers.)

10.) SAUSAGE MUFFINS

These are corn muffins with sausage in them. Uncle Joe called them "meat-breads." You can use any kind of store-bought sausage you like, but we always used home-made – we'll pass along a quick, easy recipe for that, too.

Uncle Joe's recipe:

1 (tea)spoon bake powder
1 (tea)spoon bake soda
1 half (tea)spoon salt (or to taste)
1 cup (unbleached) flour
1 cup cornmeal
2 cups sausage (chopped up)
3 eggs
1 cup buttermilk
2 table spoons light oil (nut, seed or corn oil)
Bread-cake pan (he means a muffin pan)

Heat oven good. (As I've said, I don't know how he knew how hot to get his brick oven, but set your modern oven hot, 375 to 400 degrees or so.) Chop up sausage. Beat up eggs good. Put buttermilk, eggs and oil in bowl. Mix up good. (He used a hand-whisk –- you can use a mixer at lower speed.) Put in cornmeal, flour, bake powder, bake soda and salt. Mix but not too much. (If you beat too hard the batter will be tough.) Put in sausage pieces. Stir up good (get the sausage bits evenly mixed throughout the batter.) Butter pan good (grease with butter. You can use store-bought liner papers if you want to be able to handle the cakes later, but if you're just going to put them on the plate hot then grease the pan instead.) Bake light brown. (We would say golden-brown. Remember, it's corn.) Makes one whole pan.

(If you want to make your own sausage, here is a simple way to do it:

Add a teaspoon of fine ground sage, a half cup of chopped green onions, a half teaspoon (or to taste) of salt, and fine red or black pepper to taste, to 2 pounds of ground beef or brisket. Make into patties and cook well-done in iron skillet. Drain well. These can be chopped up and used in the muffins. They're also good left as patties and eaten with eggs and fried potatoes. You can also use regular store-bought roll sausage but if you don't heat it first and drain off some of the fat it will make the muffins greasy when you bake them.)

11.) PECAN CHOPPED ROAST

This is a sweet, hot brisket you can make with beef or venison. In the old days it was sometimes buffalo. (Buffalo meat is good. It is grainy, and has a bit of a tang, but it is very lean. Hard to get nowadays, though.) We make it just spicy but you can put as much hot pepper in as you like; up to you. When you're heating up the oven put in the pecan-meat halves to roast. This will bring out more of their flavor.

Uncle Joe's recipe:

4 pounds meat (roast of beef or venison)
Big double handful pecans (just the meat – about a pound and a half)
1 (tea)spoon (fine) black pepper
1 half cup syrup (pure maple syrup)
1 hot pepper (cayenne or jalapeno – your choice)
1 clove garlic (the big smooth-tasting elephant garlic; if you use regular garlic just a few small cloves - it is stronger)
Stock (beef stock – bouillon will work, but remember it will be salty)
1 half (tea)spoon salt (or less – to taste)

Already roast pecans (the pecan meat halves.) Careful not to burn. (Should be long enough while the oven is pre-heating. Careful, though; too long will make the nuts tough and shriveled.) Salt and pepper on meat. Roast in oven (baking heat, about 350 degrees) pretty much done but not all the way (about an hour. He could get the heat just so in his old brick oven. No one ever saw him use a thermometer.) Take meat out of pan. Leave pan in oven to stay good and warm. Chop up garlic and hot pepper fine. Put garlic and hot pepper in stock. Stir up good. Chop up meat good. (Make brisket.) Put meat back in pan and spoon stock all over. Warm up (maple) syrup to pour. Spread on top (of meat.) Roast good (20 minutes.) Spread pecans on top. Good hot. (This is good with home-made bread and corn on the cob.)

12.) FISH CAKES

Here's a good way to fix pan fish like perch or crappie. You wind up with fish patties that are good with any kind of vegetables. When you have the fish chopped and ready, adjust the other ingredients to however many cups of fish you have to work with. Now, there is a mystery ingredient that Uncle Joe used in this recipe that he picked. Mama used dill weed, but if that's what Uncle Joe used, he didn't call it that, so what it was for sure has been lost in time. Don't use the seed, it is bitter; make sure it's the dried leaves of the weed. Rich-flavored baking potatoes work well for this. Roast them instead of boiling them.

Uncle Joe's recipe:

Panfish (filets-- perch or crappie. We will chop these to make 1 cup.)
1 big potato (roasted and mashed to make 2 cups)
1 cup cornmeal (we use coarse meal and don't sift it)
1 egg (we always use jumbo eggs)
Little handful (green) onions (about a dozen)
1 quarter clove garlic (remember, this is the giant-sized, mild-tasting elephant garlic)
(1 half (tea)spoon fine chopped dill weed)
1 half (tea)spoon black pepper
(Optional: 1 small hot pepper roasted and chopped fine)
Light oil
Salt to taste

Roast potato. Mash up. Chop up fish fine (he means dice.) Chop up onions and garlic real fine. Beat up egg real good (whip it until it's fluffy.) Put fish, potato, onions, egg, garlic, (dill weed,) black pepper and little bit (pinch) salt (and the optional chopped hot pepper) in big bowl. Mix good (get the seasonings mixed throughout.) Mash into cakes. (These are patties, smaller and thicker than hamburger patties.) Heat up oil in pan (a big, medium-deep iron skillet) medium hot over fire. (Don't make it sizzling hot; that will make the outside part of the fish tough before the inside gets done. Make it baking hot.) Put cornmeal in other pan. Put cakes in cornmeal and roll good (get a good complete coating.) Put cakes in pan in hot oil. Be sure to stir little bit. (Sauté. You want to keep the patties from getting stuck to the pan or getting burned spots.) Turn over. Both sides light brown. (He means golden-brown.) Drain. (We always had these with asparagus or peas. Also, dill pickles go good with them.)

13.) MUSHROOM BURGERS

This is an excellent meatloaf sort of dish that is a great way to fix beef or venison. It calls for ground meat; if you use beef have the butcher grind a good lean roast cut. Uncle Joe used wild mushrooms, but you can buy them. Try to get either button mushrooms, which have a smooth flavor, or portabella mushrooms which have a richer, meaty flavor. Fresh corn off the cob is best.

Uncle Joe's recipe:

2 pounds ground meat (good roast cut of beef or game)
Big double handful mushrooms (we will chop these to make 2 cups)
1 cup (whole kernel) corn
2 big white onions
1 big (hot) pepper
1 (tea)spoon black pepper
Salt to taste
Stock (Broth or beef bouillon)
Light oil

Chop up mushrooms. Slice onions. Cut up (hot) pepper little pieces. Heat oil in pan over fire hot. Put in mushrooms, corn, onions, (hot) pepper and black pepper. Fry quick. (He means sauté.) Stir up good. (Keep stirred so there won't be any burned spots.) Medium fire (turn down.) Make meat into cakes (this means patties.) While mushrooms cooking make clear place in middle of pan (this is an iron skillet, remember.) Cook each meat (patty. More sauté; don't let the patty stick to the skillet.) Each one is cooked both sides take out and drain. Put on bread. (Or hamburger bun. Or plate.) When all meats done put little stock (broth) in pan and scrape bottom (to get the good crispy off the bottom and mixed into the broth.) Put little salt (to taste.) Put sauce (the ingredients in the skillet) on meats. (On a bun or slice of bread this makes a great hot sandwich. Good with green beans.)

14.) SMALL-GAME FRY STEW

Here is a stew for chicken or rabbit. Like the big-game stew you brown the meat in the skillet instead of roasting it. Good also for turkey, squirrel, quail and duck. You need some stock, or broth, for this one. We brew some chicken bouillon and add milk -- remember, though, bouillon is salty, so careful when you add salt later.

Uncle Joe's recipe:

Meat from bird or (small) game (we will cut it up later – you'll need enough to make 5 to 6 pounds or so of meat)
1 half cup (unbleached) flour
1 half cup cornmeal
1 big (or 2 medium) white onion
1 bunch carrots (typical grocery-store-sized bunch, 6 or 8)
Big handful (wild or green) onions (couple dozen)
Couple mint leaves (we have used basil, or bay – your choice – if you use mint go easy. It is a strong flavor)
1 (tea)spoon) black pepper
1 (tea)spoon red pepper (or paprika)
1 half (tea)spoon (or more, to taste) salt
Stock (make up about four cups of chicken bouillon and add a cup of milk)
Light oil (remember this is nut or seed oil) enough to cover meat in pan

Cut up meat in pieces (about like half the big part of a chicken drumstick) make 5 or 6 pounds. Chop up onions fine. Cut up carrots little pieces. Chop up mint (or basil) leaf fine. Sift flour. Sift cornmeal. Put cornmeal, flour, (red and black) pepper and salt in big bowl. Mix up good. Put in meat pieces and cover (coat) with powders. Heat up oil in pan medium hot over fire. Put in meat pieces. Keep stirred. (This is sauté - keep the meats from sticking to the pan or each other or getting burned spots.) Cook (brown) outside good. Put in carrots, (green & white) onions and mint (or basil.) Stir good. Drain oil good. Put in stock (to cover ingredients.) Stir good while still hot. (Get everything blended well.) More salt if need. Low fire (turn way down.) Cover pan. Slow cook (simmer for 1 hour. This is good with any kind of bread.)

15.) SMOKED MEAT SPREAD

Here is a good spread for crackers. This uses something that has been popular with our family all my life (since the early fifties) and still is: Philadelphia cream cheese. (There may be other brands but I don't know.) Uncle Joe simply called it Philadelphia. He didn't think of it as cheese. You can even get low-fat versions, but we don't. He also used wild mushrooms, but if you don't have a source for those use the store kind. Wild or not, use button or portabella mushrooms for beef or venison, and oyster mushrooms for pork chops or poultry. You can use any kind of meat you like; this recipe works for any game or poultry. Lightly roasting the pepper and garlic before you chop them will bring out more flavor.

Uncle Joe's recipe:

1 pound meat (your choice)
1 half pound Philadelphia (cream cheese)
Handful mushrooms (we will chop these up to make ½ cup– see note above for best type)
1 half stick butter (about 2 oz)
2 (wild or green) onions
1 big hot pepper
1 quarter clove garlic (this is the giant clove from the elephant garlic)
1 (tea)spoon (black) pepper
Half (tea)spoon salt
Little bit light oil

Already smoke meat. (Slow cook the meat in the smoker. Wet some hickory chips to get good smoke. Out west mesquite is used, but since we have hickory around here that's what we use.) Not too long! only enough to make done. (You want the meat to remain tender – this is not jerky.) Heat little bit oil in pan over fire. Slice mushrooms. Put in pan to fry. Stir around (to keep them from burning or sticking.) Drain good. Put in oven (smoker) with meat to get smoke flavor, not too long. (Check on the mushrooms – you don't want to over-cook them – that will make them tough.) Put hot pepper and garlic in oven (smoker) to roast. (Again, don't over-cook.) When meat just done still tender chop up fine. (Here's where you want to make sure you haven't over-cooked the meat and that it's not dried-out. If it's too dry and tough it won't mash into spread.) Put meat in big bowl and mash up. (Use a heavy fork.) Chop up onions little pieces. Chop up (hot) pepper fine. Chop up garlic fine. Warm up butter soft but not melted. Put mushrooms, Philadelphia (cream cheese,) onions, butter, (hot) pepper and garlic in bowl with meat. Mash up good. (Make a paste. Blend ingredients thoroughly.) Put salt (to taste) and (black) pepper. Mix up. Spread on bread. (This stuff is great with those big 'scoop' dip corn chips. Also good on the cocktail crackers such as Ritzs, Hi-Hos or Club Crackers. Also good in the frybread shells from the Meat Pie recipe. Also good on a bun like sloppy-joe.)

(ADDED NOTE: You can use fish for this recipe very well. Leave out the hot pepper and put in a teaspoon of chopped dill weed and half-one of grated lemon or lemon juice.)

16.) GRILLED MEAT WITH SWEET SAUCE

Grilled meat is my idea of true food. In this recipe you can use steaks, of course, but we simply cut roast into steak-sized slabs and it works very nicely. Great also for pork chops, or chicken breasts, or prime rib, or rabbit. Uncle Joe used a wood fire to grill but charcoal is fine. Don't use gas-fired grill. The gas ruins the flavor. These ingredients will give enough grilling sauce for lots of meat.

Uncle Joe's recipe:

Meat (anything you want to grill)
1 cup (fresh) blackberries
1 cup (muscadine) grapes (you can use grocery-store grapes get the darkest, ripest ones you can find)
1 little white onion
1 bit-part garlic (this is the end of a clove of the giant elephant garlic. You can substitute a small regular clove but it's not as good)
1 cup cider (sweet cider, not vinegar cider. Apple juice will work)
1 tablespoon cornstarch
1 half (tea)spoon black pepper
1 half (tea)spoon red pepper
1 half (tea)spoon salt
Couple mint leaves
Little bit light oil (nut or seed oil)

(To make the sauce:)

Heat up oil in pan over fire medium hot. Chop up onion fine. Chop up garlic fine. Put in pan and fry little bit. Keep stirred up. (Sauté – shake the pan and don't let the ingredients stick or burn.) Mash up berries and grapes and put in pan. Mix up good. (Keep stirring.) Put cornstarch in cider (apple juice.) Stir up (till the cornstarch is dissolved. This will thicken the sauce.) Put in pan. Keep cooking (and stirring,) make thick. Not too hot. (Don't let it boil.) Chop up mint fine and put in too. Low fire (turn down.) Put in red and black pepper and salt. Slow cook (simmer) little bit (5 to 10 minutes.) Don't forget to stir. (Keep from burning.) Put on meat. (Use a brush.) Meat on fire (grill.) First side done turn over. Put sauce on other side. Cook some more. (I like mine medium rare; just a hint of pink, nice and juicy. Very good with fried corn and dinner rolls.)

17.) CHICKEN POTATO SOUP

This is another hearty soup with lots of potato. Especially rich if you use all dark chicken meat, lighter with breast meat, but we just used a whole chicken – easier to steam. The little red-skinned new potatoes have the best flavor for this. Uncle Joe used wild mushrooms, but he could get all he wanted. You can use package mushrooms from the store. Wild or not, try to find oyster mushrooms, which are a good complement for poultry. The thick stock for this soup is made by adding brewed chicken bouillon to milk. Remember, though, bouillon is salty, so careful as you add salt later.

Uncle Joe's recipe:

1 chicken (or 3-4 pounds whichever cut of chicken you like)
2 pounds red potatoes
3 middle-size tomatoes
Handful mushrooms (we will chop these to make 1 cup)
1 big white onion
Big handful (wild or green) onions (couple dozen)
6 big stalks celery
2 cups milk
Chicken stock (use chicken bouillon if you like)
1 (tea)spoon fine black pepper
Little bit salt (won't take much with the bouillon; to your taste)

Cut chicken in pieces (separate legs, breast sides, etc. if not already.) Chop up white onion. Cut up mushrooms. Put chicken pieces, mushrooms, white onion, (black) pepper and salt in deep pot. Cover with stock (bouillon.) Cover pot. Steam till chicken bones fall out (20 minutes.) Cut up chicken little pieces (bite-size.) Put in pot. Put pot back on medium fire. Cut up potatoes (1/2 inch cubes.) Put potatoes and milk in pot. More stock to cover potatoes. (Put in the milk first, then however much new heated stock to cover everything.) Cut up tomatoes (quarter the quarters.) Chop (green) onions short bits. Chop celery short bits. Put tomatoes, (green) onions and celery in pot. Cook on medium fire (till) potatoes are done, not too long. (Don't make the potatoes mushy.) Good on cold day. (This is a sort of chowder soup. It's good with sliced, whole-grain bread.)

18.) GRILLED MEAT WITH MUSHROOM SAUCE

This is about the best way there is to fix venison, but you can use it for any meat. Beef, pork chops, and chicken all come out good. Here again, Uncle Joe used wild mushrooms, but he knew where to find them. You can use package mushrooms from the store. Wild or not, use button or portabella mushrooms for beef or venison, and oyster mushrooms for pork chops or poultry. If you don't have any stock handy use bouillon to make some, but it is salty, so don't add as much salt later. Uncle Joe grilled over a wood fire but charcoal is fine. Don't use propane, though – it makes the meat taste like propane. These ingredients will make enough sauce for meat for the whole table.

Uncle Joe's recipe:

Meat (whatever you like – we particularly like either venison or beef roast slabs)
Big double handful mushrooms (we will chop these up to make about 2 pounds worth – see note above for best type)
2 big onions (red or white for beef, yellow for chicken)
1 clove garlic (the big giant clove from elephant garlic)
1 stick butter (4 oz)
1 (tea)spoon black pepper
1 (tea)spoon salt (or less – to taste)
Stock (beef or chicken. Make it with bouillon. For chicken bouillon use milk to brew)
Light oil (nut or seed oil)

Cut meat to grill. (Like steaks or chops.) Heat up grill. Heat oil and butter in big pan over medium fire. Cut up mushrooms and onions little pieces. Chop up garlic fine. Put onions, garlic and pepper in pan. Fry little bit. Keep stirred. (Sauté – stir so that there are no burned spots.) Put sauce (the sauté) from pan on meat (use a brush.) Put on grill. One side done (seared) turn over. Put mushrooms in pan. Stir up. Cook little while (10 minutes.) Keep stirred. Low fire (turn down.) Put stock (enough to cover the ingredients.) Slow cook (simmer) little while. (Cook till the mushrooms are tender.) Put salt if need. (If the stock is salty you may not need much.) Meat done good put on plate and rest of sauce (the mushrooms and other things in the pan) on top. (This is another good one with sliced, whole grain bread. Or dinner rolls. Or frybread, or grilled toast.)

SIDE DISHES

SOUPS AND VEGETABLES AND SALADS
Before you start on each section make sure you have read the introductory section at the beginning of the cookbook!

Here are some recipes which are nowadays generally considered side dishes; however, in the old days these things were often the main courses if there was no meat to be had. Corn, beans, potatoes and rice were considered the main staples of diet, as they could be raised and harvested just about anywhere, unlike game, which might or might not be available.

INGREDIENTS: Uncle Joe usually used plain old pinto beans because that's what he grew, but he also used red kidney-type beans, and of course there are other kinds available. The bottom line is in the seasoning. Uncle Joe was fond of sweet potatoes, and if that's what he means he will say sweet potatoes; regular old potatoes are simply "potatoes." He grew the old big gourd squash; if you don't have a garden (or know someone who does) you can get all kinds at the store. The best are either butternut or buttercup – those are the sweetest. Mama called both kinds butter-squash. Fresh corn is always better. Think about how good boiled corn-on-the-cob is compared to canned pre-cooked whole kernel corn. All the difference in the world. Roasted is even better. Most of us don't have the opportunity to collect wild mushrooms, but here is one place where you can get reasonably close with store-bought, if they are pretty fresh. Portabella mushrooms are rich and meaty-tasting. The little button mushrooms are smoother. If garlic is called for it is the giant elephant garlic, which is smoother-tasting than regular small white garlic. Well worth the effort to find. An elephant clove is as big as a whole bulb of the white kind, but the white kind is stronger and not as smooth. If you can get garden tomatoes those are best. The store tomatoes don't have much taste anymore.

Here are all kinds of good things from Uncle Joe's kitchen, with our own introductions, and with our own comments and clarifications in parentheses:

1.) SWEET CORN STUFFING
2.) SQUASH MUSHROOM HASH
3.) HOT BEAN SALAD
4.) SQUASH & CORN
5.) CORN BEAN DUMPLINGS
6.) SPICE CORN PUDDING
7.) RICE & SQUASH
8.) COLD BEAN SALAD
9.) POTATO CORN SOUP
10.) BEAN SQUASH SOUP
11.) SCRAMBLED PEPPER EGGS
12.) CHOKE-NUT SALAD
13.) ROAST PUMPKIN SEEDS

1.) SWEET CORN STUFFING

This is what we fixed for a good dressing to go with meat or eat by itself. Don't use sweet milk instead of buttermilk. Buttermilk is worth the trouble to get. Lightly roast the corn ahead of time for more flavor.

Uncle Joe's recipe:

1 (tea)spoon bake powder
2 cups corn (fresh roasted kernels off the cob)
1 cup cornmeal (coarse)
1 quarter cup (unbleached) flour
1 and half cups buttermilk
2 big eggs
Little handful (wild or green) onions (about a dozen)
1 half sweet red pepper (he means a red bell pepper)
1 quarter clove garlic (this is the giant, smooth-tasting elephant garlic.)
1 middle size hot pepper not a real hot one (green chili works good)
1 tablespoon syrup (he used pure maple syrup; honey is smoother but maple syrup has a nice tang)
1 (tea)spoon (ground) sage
1 (tea)spoon salt (or less – to taste)
4 tablespoons oil (corn oil is fine)

Heat up oven medium hot. (Here we are back to baking. Uncle Joe could get his old brick wood-fired oven just the right heat, but nobody really knows how he did. Make it a good baking heat, 350 degrees.) Chop up onions little. Chop up sweet pepper little. Chop up garlic and hot pepper fine. (Dice.) Beat up eggs. Warm up syrup (or honey) to pour. Put everything (all ingredients) in big bowl. Mix good. (Make sure all ingredients are thoroughly mixed, with no lumps.) Butter pan. (He used earthenware baking pans; glass or good heavy iron will work. He used butter to grease with.) Bake good (1 hour.) Check with fork. (Fork should come out of the center clean.) Crumble up. (Eat it now steamy hot as dressing, or:) Spread out to dry (and use as stuffing; very good in chicken or turkey.)

2.) SQUASH MUSHROOM HASH

This is a kind of hash dish with mushrooms, squash and corn, a little bit spicy. Uncle Joe used wild mushrooms, of course. He knew where to find them and which ones to pick. At the store you can get portabella mushrooms, which are rich and sort of meaty tasting, or little button mushrooms, which are the old classic smooth mushroom taste. Or, if this dish is to go with a poultry dish, oyster mushrooms are good. For squash the best is butternut or buttercup. Those are the sweetest. There is cheese in this recipe. Uncle Joe used locally produced, in big chunks. Our favorite kind has always been longhorn-style Colby, because it is rich and smooth. Don't use sharp cheddar; you want a smooth taste to go with the mushrooms.

Big handful mushrooms (enough to make 1 cup when cut up into bits)

1 cup corn (whole fresh kernels off the cob)

2 medium (or 4 little) squash (Enough of whatever kind you use to make about 4 cups of cut-up small pieces)

Handful-size fresh cheese (this will be about 4 ounces. Make about a half-cup when grated)

Handful (wild or green) onions (couple dozen)

1 quarter clove garlic (giant elephant garlic clove)

Little tomato (to make quarter to third cup chopped up)

1 middle size hot pepper (cayenne pepper)

Stock (broth – bouillon will work. Beef for beef or game, chicken for poultry. It will take about a half cup)

1 half (tea)spoon black pepper

1 half (tea)spoon salt (or less - to taste – the bouillon is salty)

Butter to cook

Good heavy pan (deep iron skillet)

Cut up squash, mushrooms and tomato little pieces. Chop up onion. Chop up garlic and hot pepper fine (dice.) Heat up pan medium hot. Melt butter in pan. Put in squash, mushrooms, corn and onions. Quick fry. Keep stirred up good. (This is sauté. Keep stirred to prevent burned spots.) Cook but not too much. (Cooking too long will not only burn but make the squash and mushrooms tough.) Put in stock (broth,) tomato, garlic, hot pepper, black pepper and salt. Stir up good. Cook little longer (another 5 minutes.) Grate cheese. Put on (spread on top.) Low fire (turn down.) Slow cook. (Low heat – simmer for ten minutes or so.) When cheese gets warm take off fire. (Watch for the cheese to melt but not get tough and gummy. You want it to stay on top as a cover.) Good with meat. (This is very good with hot roast sandwiches or with hamburgers. Also with roast turkey – for that remember to use chicken broth and oyster mushrooms.)

3.) HOT BEAN SALAD

This means served hot, not pepper hot, although you could pepper it up if you like. Uncle Joe used 'greens.' This could be mustard greens, collard greens, polk salad or spinach. He used whatever he got from the garden or wild. If you don't have a garden or access to wild greens then about as easy as anything is just get some spinach leaves from the store. Any kind of beans will work, of course, but he (and we) used plain old pinto beans. You need to plan to cook them ahead of time so they will be ready when you start to build the salad. You can use any kind of nuts, but we all think pecans are the best.

Uncle Joe's recipe:

2 big handfuls greens (cut spinach or other leaves in cross-sections to make about 2 quarts)

1 cup beans

Handful pecans (chop pecan meats to make about a quarter cup)

1 little purple (or red) onion

Few (about 3 or 4) (wild or green) onions

1 sweet red pepper (he means a red bell pepper)

1 half cup sweet vinegar (he means apple cider vinegar)

1 tablespoon syrup (this is pure maple syrup – no sugar added!)

1 half (tea)spoon black pepper

Little bit (pinch) salt (this is to taste – start conservative)

Light oil (light flower oil is best)

Good heavy (iron) pan

Already slow cook beans. Cut up greens bite size. Chop up pecans. Chop up (green) onions little pieces (not too fine.) Also chop up sweet pepper little pieces. Slice up purple onion thin. Break up slices. Warm up syrup to pour. Put greens in big bowl. Heat oil in bottom of pan medium hot. Put in pecans and cook but not too long. (Just heat them up warm; if you cook too long they'll get tough.) Drain. Put in bowl with greens. Put all onions in pan. Cook but not brown. (Just heat them up warm.) Stir up good. Drain. Put in with greens. Put beans and sweet pepper in pan. May need little bit oil. Cook but not too much. Remember to stir. (Don't cook too long or the beans will burn and the pepper pieces will get tough. Keep them stirred. Remember, the beans are already cooked.) Drain (oil from pan.) Put in (cider) vinegar and syrup. Stir up. Put in big bowl with greens. Put in black pepper and salt. Stir up good with forks (here he means toss the salad.) Eat warm. (This is really good with garlic bread.)

4.) SQUASH & CORN

Although considered a vegetable dish, corn is actually fruit. In fact, each kernel is a complete, miniature fruit. Squash is actually a berry. All the same to me. Remember: use fresh kernels off the cob – much better than canned. Here again the best squash is either butternut or buttercup. They are the sweetest. Use yellow onion with this recipe. For stock you can use bouillon or broth from another dish. Chicken works best for this. It is smoother than beef stock. If you use bouillon, remember it might be pretty salty.

Uncle Joe's recipe:

4 cups corn (4 cups of fresh kernels off the cob)

2 medium (or 4 little) squash (Enough of whatever kind you use to make about 4 cups of cut-up small pieces)

1 sweet red pepper (this is a red bell pepper)

1 big yellow onion

Little handful (wild or green) onions (about a dozen)

1 quarter clove garlic (the giant elephant garlic)

Stock (chicken broth or bouillon – shouldn't take much)

1 half (tea)spoon black pepper

1 half (tea)spoon salt (or less – to taste – the bouillon will be salty)

Light oil

Good heavy (iron) pan

Cut up squash little pieces. Chop up sweet pepper, garlic and all onions. Heat up oil in pan medium hot. Quick fry onions, garlic and sweet pepper. (He means sauté, about 5 minutes.) Remember to stir. (Don't let any stick or burn.) Put in squash and corn. Stir up good. Cook little bit more (about another 5 minutes.) Drain. Low fire (turn way down.) Put in stock (enough to cover the ingredients.) Put in pepper and salt. Stir up good. Cover up. Slow cook (simmer till) everything tender but not too much (about 15 minutes. Don't overcook or the corn gets mushy and the other ingredients get tough.) Good warm.

5.) CORN BEAN DUMPLINGS

These are little dumplings to go in the soup pot. You need to cook the beans ahead of time. Then, assemble the ingredients while your soup – whatever kind it is – is simmering. When you have them ready, you will drop them in the soup when it has another 15 minutes or so to cook. This makes a soup dish a lot more substantial. We have always used pinto beans, mainly because we just always have, but kidney beans are good, too. This is enough for a big pot; we always make soup for more than one supper.

Uncle Joe's recipe:

2 (tea)spoons bake powder
2 cups cornmeal
1 half cup (unbleached) flour
1 cup beans
1 cup milk
4 eggs
Few (wild or green) onions (about a half dozen)
1 half (tea)spoon black pepper
1 half (tea)spoon salt
2 tablespoons oil (corn oil is good)

Cook beans already. Sift cornmeal and flour good and fine. Beat up eggs good. Chop up onions little pieces. Put everything (all ingredients in recipe) in big bowl. Dip little stock (the broth) out of soup and put in. (Add to batter.) Mix up good. (Beat to make batter smooth. Add broth until you have enough so the batter will mix smooth. Uncle Joe used a hand whisk; use your mixer on lower speed.) Big tablespoon of batter (mix) in hot (simmering) soup. (Put batter mix in one spoon at a time.) Careful not to splash. Dumplings will cook with soup. (This will turn soup into a pretty big meal. Good with green beans on the side.)

6.) SPICE CORN PUDDING

This is a good side dish that you use instead of creamed corn or sweet potatoes. Roast the sweet potatoes in the recipe ahead of time so they will be ready when you put this dish together. If you have a pepper grinder then fresh-ground peppercorns are best. If you buy it already ground then get fine-ground for this dish. The giant elephant garlic is much better than the regular white kind; it is smoother-tasting. Uncle Joe used home-made apple wine that he called 'sweet cider.' It was very sweet. It was also very strong. Store-bought cider is not as sweet; we just used apple juice, and mixing in a little white grape juice is good, too. Roasting the sweet potato brings out more flavor.

Uncle Joe's recipe:

1 cup (fresh, whole-kernel) corn
1 half cup (roasted and mashed) sweet potato
1 cup cornmeal
Few (wild or green) onions (about half dozen)
1 quart sweet cider (use apple juice or even better 3 parts apple to 1 part white grape juice)
1 quarter clove garlic (giant elephant garlic)
1 half stick butter
1 half (tea)spoon (fine) red pepper
1 half (tea)spoon (fine) black pepper
1 quarter (tea)spoon (ground) cinnamon
Little salt (to taste)

Already roast sweet potato. (Not too long or it will get tough.) Sift cornmeal good and fine. Chop up onions little pieces. Chop up garlic fine. Mash up sweet potato. Heat up pot (deep skillet or good heavy saucepan) medium hot and melt butter. Put in garlic to quick fry. (He means sauté.) Don't burn (remember to stir.) Put in sweet potato and cider (juice.) Stir up good. Low fire (turn down.) Put in corn, cornmeal, salt, (red and black) pepper and cinnamon. Stir up good. Slow cook little while (simmer 10 minutes.) Stir. Cover up and take off fire. Let cool little bit (to be firm) but still warm. Scoop out. Put onion on top. (Sprinkle the uncooked chopped onion on top of servings.) Good by itself. (It does make a good snack, as well as a good side dish to go with any kind of meat.)

7.) RICE & SQUASH

This is a good rice dish with lots of different flavors. The main thing is: don't use bleached, white rice. No flavor, no nutrient value. Use long grain brown rice, or wild rice. The sweet butter-types of squash are always good, but this is a good place to mix in also some plain old regular squash, like zucchini. We use pinto beans, which makes for a substantial taste, but if you want a lighter, more vegetable-type taste you can use lima beans. Uncle Joe was partial to the red bell peppers, but we like to use both red and green ones. Use fresh corn kernels off the cob, much better than canned. This garlic is the giant elephant garlic. It is smoother tasting than regular white garlic. Each clove is as big as a whole bulb of the smaller kind. Roasting the garlic, corn and sweet pepper ahead of time brings out more flavor. Remember to cook the beans ahead of time, too, so they'll be ready.

Uncle Joe's recipe:

1 cup rice

2 cups (fresh, whole kernel) corn

2 cups beans (either kind – see notes)

2 squash (cut up in little pieces to make 2 cups – we like 1 cup of sweet buttercup or butternut squash and 1 cup of a plain squash like zucchini)

2 sweet red peppers (bell peppers – we use 1 green and 1 red)

1 middle size white onion

Few (wild or green) onions (about a half dozen)

1 half clove garlic (this is the giant elephant garlic)

1 quarter (tea)spoon black pepper

1 quarter (tea)spoon red pepper

Little salt

Stock (chicken broth – you can use chicken bouillon. Start with about 4 cups, and have more on hand just in case. Bouillon is salty – watch how much salt you add later.)

Light oil (you can use corn oil, but this is a good place for a flower oil like canola or peanut – it gets crispy hot better than the heavier oils.)

Good deep pot. (The heavier the better.)

Already cook beans. Cut up sweet peppers little strips. Roast corn, peppers and garlic in oven little bit. Cut up squash little pieces. Chop up all onions. Chop up (roasted) garlic fine. Heat up stock in pot good and hot then medium fire (turn down.) Put in rice with little salt. (Just a pinch!) Cover. Let cook. (Remember, rice takes a while. Let it steam for 20 minutes or so.) Keep stirred. (Stir it so you don't get any burned spots on the bottom layer.) Put in corn, beans and squash. Stir up good. Cover and cook more. (More steaming; another 15 or 20 minutes.) Heat little bit oil in pan (iron skillet) medium hot. (Enough oil to coat the bottom of the skillet well.) Put in sweet peppers, onions and garlic. Quick fry (stir fry) but not too done. (Don't brown the ingredients.) Put in red and black pepper. Stir up good. Put everything (from pan) in rice pot and stir up good. May need to put in little stock. Maybe little salt (to taste.) Cover and steam little bit (few more minutes.) Stir up (fluff the rice.) Good with chicken. (It is, with roast or baked chicken or turkey, or with pork chops.)

8.) COLD BEAN SALAD

This is actually a bean side dish that goes about anywhere you need a salad. It can sit out all afternoon without going bad and tastes just as good later. This is not a light dinner salad; it is substantial. It is good with garlic bread. Again, Uncle Joe liked the red bell peppers; we also use green ones. Use one of each. Using different kinds of beans together gives a nice flavor combination, but you cook them separately so that the flavors will be unique until they are blended in the recipe. Plan to have them cooked ahead of time. Use the giant elephant garlic. This is one place he liked honey instead of syrup.

Uncle Joe's recipe:

2 cups green beans
2 cups red kidney beans
2 cups pinto beans
2 sweet red peppers (bell peppers. Use 1 red and 1 green)
1 big purple onion
Handful (wild or green) onions (about a dozen)
1 third clove garlic (giant elephant garlic)
1 half cup cider vinegar (if you use bottled vinegar get the darkest sweetest variety)
1 half cup honey
1 big hot (cayenne) pepper
1 half (tea)spoon rough (coarse-ground) black pepper
1 half (tea)spoon salt (or more – to taste)
1 half cup light oil (sunflower oil is good

Already cook 3 kinds beans separate in 3 pots (or in the same pot at three different times.) Slice purple onion thin and break up slices. (Break slices by hand so that you have little crescent-shaped bits.) Chop up (wild) onions little pieces (quarter-inch bits.) Cut up sweet peppers little pieces. Chop up garlic fine. Chop up hot pepper fine. Put all beans, onions and sweet peppers in big bowl. Mix up good. Warm up honey to pour. Put honey, garlic, cider (vinegar), hot pepper, black pepper and salt in little bowl. Mix up good. Put in oil and mix up good. Mixed up good and even put in big bowl. Stir up with forks. (Here he means to toss it rather than stir it around.) Good for snack. (Mama always said that putting it in the ice box to get cold would make it taste better later. She would leave it all morning to blend the flavors together. Then you can eat it cold or let it warm to room temperature to eat. Good at family reunions and picnics.)

9.) POTATO CORN SOUP

This is good, thick soup. You put meat in it, and about any kind you like will work. Most often we use bacon or cubes of ham. Also good is turkey breast or chicken. You make the corn cream-style this way: after you cut the kernels off the cob you use the knife to scrape the cob and get the pulpy bases of the kernels off. That material goes in with the kernels, and when you cook it you get the creamy texture. The sweet yellow onions are best with this. Stock means broth – we use chicken broth or chicken bouillon. I like more black pepper in it, but start with the recipe – you can always add more. This is great with those buttery snack crackers like Ritz, Hi-Hos or Club Crackers.

Uncle Joe's recipe:

1 quarter pound ham (or 1 half pound bacon)
3 big potatoes
2 cups corn (fresh whole kernel off the cob – remember to include the pulp – see note above)
1 quart milk (NOT SKIM!)
1 quart stock (broth – bouillon will work)
1 big yellow onion
1 (tea)spoon (or less) black pepper
Little salt (pinch --won't take much. The meat and the broth will both be salty)
Oil to cook (corn oil is fine)

Cut up meat in bite pieces (3/8 inch cubes. Or, if you use bacon, chop it.) Also potatoes in bite pieces (more small cubes.) Chop up onion fine (dice.) Heat up oil in pan pretty hot. Put in meat. Quick fry (brown.) Keep stirred. (Don't burn.) Low fire little bit. Put in onion. Stir up (sauté - don't let it burn.) Put stock in pot. Raise up fire, almost boil. (Slow, rolling boil.) Put in meat, onion and potatoes. Careful not to splash! Keep almost boil until potatoes stirred in good. Low fire (turn way down) and slow cook (simmer.) Keep stirred. Make potatoes almost done. (This means a little soft but not mushy – check them with a fork. 30 or 40 minutes.) Put in corn and milk. Stir good. Slow cook (20 minutes. He didn't usually specify times, but 20 minutes is about right.) Keep stirred. Salt and pepper (to taste.) Good with crackers. (I don't know if he knew about Ritz but I bet he'd approve them for use. Also good with biscuits.)

10.) BEAN SQUASH SOUP

This is a good, rich vegetable soup that is really good with cornbread. Use fresh beans. Canned ones already have all the flavor cooked out of them. Uncle Joe usually used regular old pinto beans for just about everything, but red beans are good too. He grew green and lima beans (which he called butterbeans, although those are actually something else.) He used home-grown gourd squash; we always use either buttercup or butternut squash. Those are the sweetest. Yellow onions are best, I think, in this dish. (He thought so, too.) When he calls for stock he means broth; you can use bouillon if you don't have any broth handy, but bouillon is salty so be careful when you're adding salt later. When he says sweet peppers he means bell peppers. He was partial to the red ones, but we use red and green and sometimes yellow; they are a little different in taste and give a bit of variety. Remember to cook the pinto or red beans beforehand because they take a while.

Uncle Joe's recipe:

1 big squash (you want enough to make about 2 cups cubed)
1 cup beans (we like red beans for this)
1 cup butterbeans (regular old lima beans are what we use)
3 cups corn (whole fresh kernels off the cob)
1 handful green beans (he means fresh-picked, of course. Cut enough to make a cup.)
2 sweet red peppers (bell peppers – use 1 red and 1 yellow or green)
1 big yellow onion (or 2 medium ones)
2 quarts stock (beef or chicken broth. You probably won't use it all, but it's handy for other things, too)
1 (tea)spoon (ground) sage
1 half (tea)spoon black pepper
1 half (tea)spoon red pepper
1 half (tea)spoon salt (or to taste)
Oil for cooking (little bit for sautéing – you can use butter)
Good heavy pot (iron soup pot)
(AND: Mama liked to put in a leaf of mint sometimes. Just a little; don't make it mint soup. Bay leaves are good, too; I don't think Uncle Joe had them but I'm not sure)

Cook beans already. (Beans take longer than the corn, green beans and lima beans so they need to be already cooked when you start the recipe.) Cut up green beans and squash. Chop up onion and peppers. Heat little oil in pot medium hot. Put in onion and peppers. Quick fry. (This means sauté. If you do this the onion and pepper pieces will have just little bit of crispness and won't get soggy in the soup.) Keep stirred (don't burn.) Put in stock (broth.) Put in sage, red and black pepper and salt. Stir up good. Put in all other things (rest of ingredients – the corn, squash and all the beans.) one at a time. Careful not to splash. Stir good each new part (ingredient.) Good hot fire (almost boiling.) Stir some more (make sure all ingredients are well-blended.) Low fire (turn down) and slow cook (cover and simmer.) Good hot soup on cold day. (Don't forget the cornbread.)

11.) SCRAMBLED PEPPER EGGS

These go good with sausage or ham or bacon, and also good with hot biscuits. Our hens laid the brown speckled eggs, which taste better, but any kind will work. Nowadays I like to get jumbo-sized ones, and it seems like they taste better, too, but that might be my imagination. If you roast the bell peppers before cooking the recipe they will have a bit of crispness to them and not get tough, but only if you don't over-cook them when you roast them. Roasting brings out more flavor. The garlic in this is the giant elephant garlic, which has a smoother, milder taste than regular white garlic. Well worth the effort to find. He had a giant-sized iron griddle-pan that would cook a dozen eggs easily, but we have re-sized the recipe for normal skillets, so we halved the amounts.

Uncle Joe's (re-sized) recipe:

1 half doz big eggs
1 big tomato
2 sweet red peppers (red bell peppers)
1 half clove garlic (the giant elephant garlic clove)
Big handful (wild or green) onions (couple dozen)
1 big hot (cayenne) pepper
1 (tea)spoon syrup (pure maple syrup)
1 half (tea)spoon black pepper
1 half (tea)spoon (ground) sage
1 half (tea)spoon salt
Oil for cooking (corn oil is fine)
Good heavy pan (deep iron skillet)

Already roast peppers, not too long (don't make them tough.) Cut up sweet peppers, onions and tomato little pieces. Chop up hot pepper and garlic fine (dice.) Warm up syrup (or honey) to pour. Heat little bit oil in pan good and hot. Put in sweet peppers, hot pepper, onions and garlic. Quick fry. (He means sauté. Keep it stirred so there are no burned spots.) Low fire (turn way down.) Put in tomato, syrup (or honey,) sage, black pepper and salt. Slow cook. (Over low heat till thoroughly warmed.) Medium fire (turn up.) Break in eggs. (Break in bowl to pour in.) Be ready to stir quick (scramble fast to get the ingredients blended in before the eggs get hard.) Good with frybread. (My favorite with these is still biscuits. Good for breakfast, dinner, supper or late-night snack.)

12.) SWEET-SOUR CHOKE-NUT SALAD

Here is a salad that uses what Uncle Joe called choke-root. They are a plant similar to artichokes, and are sometimes called Jerusalem artichokes. They are also known as sweet-chokes, or sun-chokes. When he specified greens, he wasn't really being specific. He was liable to use polk greens, mustard greens, turnip greens or fresh spinach. Spinach or mustard greens work best. He generally used only the red bell peppers, which he called sweet red peppers, but we grew up using yellow and green ones, too. The differences in taste are subtle, but they are different, and the colors make it festive. He loved golden-delicious apples, calling them 'yellow apples.' You can also use red-delicious if you get sweet ones – generally, the darker they are the sweeter. The cider that he used was home-brewed, very potent. We use sweet, dark cider-vinegar, but you need to add some honey. Plan to cook the beans ahead of time, since they take a while. The garlic is the giant elephant garlic, which is milder and smoother than small, white garlic. Grated lemon peel is the very thin outermost skin of the lemon. Fine-grated it is called 'zest.' Don't get any of the whiter, inner peel – that part is bitter. Make it with a fine-holed grater. Finally, if you can find wild watercress it adds a sweet, pure sort of flavor. By the time it gets to the store all the flavor is gone, so if you don't know any place to pick it, then using store-bought won't add much, as far as I'm concerned. It grows wild in spring-fed pools, and very nice if you know where some is.

Uncle Joe's recipe:

Double handful pecans (shell enough to make 1 pound of meat)
2 big yellow apples
Double handful choke-root (sweet- or sun-chokes; slice enough to make 2 cups)
3 sweet red peppers (these are bell peppers – use 1 each medium-sized red, yellow and green)
1 cup red beans
Big bunch greens (mustard greens or fresh spinach – cut up enough for 1-1/2 to 2 qts)
Bunch watercress (IF you can find fresh)
1 half clove garlic (the giant elephant garlic)
Few (wild or green) onions (about a half dozen)
1 half cup cider (this is dark, sweet cider vinegar)
1 half cup syrup (he used maple syrup but honey blends better and is lighter)
1 (tea)spoon lemon peel fine (fine-grated, just the colored skin – see note)
1 quarter (tea)spoon black pepper
Light oil (flower or seed oil for the dressing – about a cup)
Little bit (pinch) salt
(Mama also added a couple of things: she liked to use dill weed, diced very fine, about a tablespoon, and she added a quarter cup of yellow mustard. You can use the richer brown or European-style mustard, which is not as pungent; use twice as much.)
To fix:

Cook beans already. Chop up garlic and lemon peel fine. (Grate the lemon peel – see note above.) Chop up pecans, greens, watercress and onions little pieces. Cut apples, choke-root and sweet peppers quarter-slices (slice thin then quarter the slices. Don't use the cores, of course.) Warm up syrup (honey) to pour. For sauce (he meant the dressing) mix oil, cider, garlic, syrup, lemon (peel), black pepper and salt (and dill and mustard) in bowl. Stir up good (blend ingredients well.) Put pecans, apples, choke-root, greens, sweet peppers, beans, onions and watercress in big bowl. Stir up good (toss.) Put sauce (dressing) in big bowl and stir up good (toss.) Let sit for flavor. (Let it marinate. The longer the better.)

13.) ROASTED PUMPKIN SEEDS

One of Dad's favorite snacks. Here's where you use the seeds you saved from one of the pumpkin recipes. We always had a bag of these in the truck when I was a kid. Easy to make, and very tasty.

Uncle Joe's recipe:

Fresh pumpkin (for the seeds – just use the ones you've saved from when you cooked the pumpkin for another recipe.)

Little bit garlic (this is the giant elephant garlic. Dice enough for about half a teaspoon)

1 half (tea)spoon salt

Big pinch black pepper

Big pinch ginger

1 half little hot (cayenne) pepper

Light oil (seed or flower or nut oil)

Already scrape pumpkin seeds. (He means remove them from the pumpkin and separate from the pulp. You'll want to roast them a double handful at a time – between 1 and 2 cups.) Heat up oven good and hot. (Once again, I don't know how he knew how hot his old wood-fired brick oven was, with no thermometer, but he always had it just right. Set yours for baking heat – 375 degrees is fine.) Roast hot pepper and garlic. (Don't make them over-dry and leathery; just get them to where they won't be wet and mushy when you dice them.) Chop up hot pepper and garlic (when roasted) real fine (fine as you can get it.) Grind up black pepper fine. (Fine-ground from the store will work.) Put hot pepper, garlic, black pepper, salt, ginger and little bit (couple of tablespoons) light oil in bowl. Stir up good. (Blend thoroughly.) Put in seeds and stir up good. (Get seeds well-coated with seasoning.) Spread seeds on pan (cookie sheet.) Put in to roast. Make crisp. (You're looking for a pretty golden-brown. This will take maybe twenty minutes; depends on how big the seeds are. Listen for them to start crackling. Don't over-roast; they'll get tough.) Good snack. (You eat them hulls and all and I've eaten a jillion of them. Also, another way to cook them is to use about a half teaspoon of chili powder instead of the hot pepper.)

Before you start on each section make sure you have read the introductory section at the beginning of the cookbook!

Some fruit/vegetable butters are sweet like jams, and some are sweet-tart to use with meat dishes. Many, many variations possible. All good.

Each recipe has our own introduction and our comments and clarifications in parentheses.

1.) SWEET POTATO BUTTER
2.) PERSIMMON SPREAD
3.) BERRY PLUM BUTTER
4.) SWEET PUMPKIN BUTTER
5.) BERRY SYRUP

1.) SWEET POTATO BUTTER

Roasted sweet potatoes are good and sweet. This butter is great to put on fresh, hot home-made bread. Leave the peels on the potato and apple because they add both flavor and nutrients. Here's that mystery ingredient that we all think must have been cloves. Nobody is sure now what he called it but it did exist.

Uncle Joe's recipe:

1 big sweet potato
1 little green apple (use a tart baking apple)
1 half (tea)spoon syrup (pure maple syrup)
Pinch fine (fine-ground) black pepper
Pinch (ground) cinnamon
Pinch (ground cloves)
Pinch salt

Put potato on grill over good hot fire. (You can bake it in the oven – set it for 425 degrees.) Remember to poke with fork. (A hole or two will keep it from blowing up!) Bake halfway (about 20 minutes – it won't be done yet.) Poke apple too. (Not a bunch of holes, just a couple to let off excess pressure.) Take out core. Put in with sweet potato (the apple, not the core.) Bake rest of way. (Careful though: if you let them cook too long the peels will get tough, especially on the potato. You want them to just get soft. Keep checking.) Let cool to handle. Put in big bowl. Mash up good. (He hand-mashed everything with a wooden pestle. We put the ingredients through a food-processor.) Warm up syrup to pour. Put in syrup, black pepper, salt, cinnamon and (cloves.) Mix up good. (Blend in the food-processor.) Good on frybread. (We use it warm but it is pretty good out of the refrigerator, too, although when it's cold it's harder to spread.)

2.) PERSIMMON SPREAD

This is a sweet-tart sauce (mostly tart) that is good with fish or poultry. You can serve it with any game, really, but it seems like we have always had it with panfish or turkey. The recipe calls for ripe persimmons. There is a reason for that. Persimmons that aren't quite ripe will give you lockjaw. They will make your nose numb. Make sure they're ripe. He used a pickle in the recipe. You can use a couple tablespoons of fresh dill weed instead, but the pickle adds to the texture of the sauce. What he calls a sweet pepper is a red bell pepper. We like to use a green one here because the flavor is a little sweeter and crisper.

Uncle Joe's recipe:

Double handful persimmons (RIPE ones! Chop enough to make a cupful. Did I mention that they need to be ripe?)
1 middle size sour pickle (he means a dill pickle)
1 little sweet pepper (a green bell pepper – chop enough to make about a half cup)
Half a little red onion (chop enough to make about a quarter cup)
1 quarter cup syrup (pure maple syrup)
1 (tea)spoon (ground) ginger
Good heavy (iron) pot

Cut up persimmons little pieces. Chop up sweet pepper, pickle and onion. Put in pot over low fire. Put in syrup and ginger. Stir up good. Cook but not too much. (Don't leave too long or the onion and pepper will get tough and the syrup will get caramelized. About 15 minutes.) Keep stirring. (You don't want burned parts.) Take off fire and put away to let sit. (Cover this up and refrigerate it till the next day. The flavors will blend together and it won't taste like separate ingredients in the same bowl.) Good with bird. (He was liable to have chicken, turkey, goose, duck, quail, pheasant, dove, and maybe some others, too.)

3.) BERRY PLUM BUTTER

Uncle Joe (and my folks) grew plums that were sweeter than the ones you get in the stores now. If you use store-bought, get the darkest, purplest one you can find, as ripe as you can find without being mushy. (Then fix them pretty soon.) Or, you can substitute nectarines. (Store peaches don't have much flavor.) The best berries, I think, are blackberries or muscadine grapes (pronounced 'MUSky-dine.') These are wild grapes that grow in the south and are very sweet. You can buy grapes at the store, but good luck finding any with any taste, so use blackberries. It is possible to use frozen berries, I suppose, but why anyone would want to is beyond me. Safest way is to pick blackberries or muscadines, or mulberries are good, too, but you have to get them in that short period after they turn ripe and before the birds and squirrels get them – they don't have thorns for protection like blackberries do. Raspberries are good too, if you live where they grow; same with blueberries. All of them interchangeable. Or you can mix and match.

Uncle Joe's recipe:

Handful plums (about 3 good-sized ones)
1 cup berries (your favorite kind or combination)
1 cup apple juice (the tartness blends with the sweet berries)
1 half cup syrup (pure maple syrup – no sugar added!)
1 quarter cup lemon juice (fresh is better than bottled)
Good heavy (iron) pot

Heat up fire medium hot. Take seeds out of plums. Put syrup, apple juice and lemon juice in pot. Stir up. Put in plums and berries (do not cut up the plums or berries.) Keep stirred! (Stir to keep from burning.) When plums and berries getting soft mash up. (Use a big spoon back to mash everything as it's cooking.) Cook good. Not too much. (Here again, overcooking makes the peels tough. Should be about 15 minutes.) Take off fire. Mash up good and stir. (He used a wooden pestle. Just put everything in a food processor or blender.) Good on biscuits. (You bet. Cold berry-butter on hot biscuit is the tops.)

4.) SWEET PUMPKIN BUTTER

Pumpkins are naturally very sweet. This simple butter is a good topping for wherever you might use cow butter or jam. When you cut open the baked pumpkin, remember to save the seeds for the roasted seeds recipe.

Uncle Joe's recipe:

1 little pumpkin
Handful pecans (shell enough to make 1 quarter cup of meat)
1 quarter cup syrup (pure maple syrup)
1 half (tea)spoon (ground) cinnamon

Heat up oven good (baking hot. He never used a thermometer on his old, wood-fired brick oven but he knew how to get it just right. Set yours on medium bake, about 375 degrees.) Poke holes in pumpkin. (Use a long-tined fork to put some holes in the pumpkin or it will blow up when it gets hot. Not lots of holes, but at least a few.) Put in oven. Bake good (about 30 minutes.) Let cool to handle. Cut in half. Scoop out middle (meat) with no seeds. (Save the seeds!) Mash (crush to paste) pecans. Warm up syrup to pour. Put pumpkin, pecans, syrup and cinnamon in heavy bowl. Mash up good. (He hand mashed with a wooden pestle; just put everything in a blender or food processor and puree.) Good on frybread. (Real good on hot banana nut bread.)

5.) FRUIT OR BERRY SYRUP

Here's a good simple way to make your own syrup for pancakes, waffles or biscuits. Cooking your favorite fruit or berries with maple syrup produces a strong, rich topping. You can use blackberries, muscadines, mulberries, blueberries, raspberries, strawberries, plums, peaches, pears or sweet apples.

Uncle Joe's recipe:

2 good cups handy berries (he used whatever was available. If you use berries, get good solid cupfuls but don't crush them in the cup. If you use fruit, cut it into berry-sized pieces to make 2 cups.)

1 cup syrup (pure maple syrup – not the kind with sugar added)

(NOTE: if you use apples, or if the fruit or berries you use aren't particularly sweet, use 1 half cup honey with 1 half cup syrup. That will make it a little smoother and sweeter to balance any sourness in the fruit or berries.)

1 quarter (tea)spoon (ground) cinnamon

Good heavy (iron) pot (or deep skillet)

Put everything in pot with little (about half a cup) water. Put on low fire. Slow cook (simmer.) Keep stirred (to keep from burning.) Don't cook too much. (If you over-cook the berry skins will get tough. Get the skins soft but not mushy, and the juice should be thick.) Mash up (puree to spread.) Good on cakes. (He means hot cakes. Also good on biscuits.)

DESSERTS

Before you start on each section make sure you have read the introductory section at the beginning of the cookbook!

At last, desserts. My favorite.

Here's where baking skills show up. I told about how Uncle Joe used a wood-fired brick oven, and how he didn't have a thermometer, and how he always got his heat just right. He will specify 'medium fire,' or 'good and hot' or whatever; we will tell you how we set our modern oven. As with all the other recipes, we use natural ingredients. Desserts are supposed to be sweet, of course. DON'T USE WHITE TABLE SUGAR. These desserts are sweetened with pure (NO SUGAR ADDED!) maple syrup or with honey. Fruits, especially dried fruits, and whole grains have plenty of natural sweetness. Throw in natural sweetener like honey or maple syrup and I guarantee it will be nice and sweet. If you use processed sugar you simply get something that tastes like processed sugar. Once you eat naturally sweetened goodies you will be converted.

Each one of Uncle Joe's recipes will have our own introduction and our own comments and clarifications in parentheses.

1.) CARROT CAKE MUFFINS
2.) BUTTER PECAN COOKIES
3.) STRAWBERRY CAKE
4.) LEMON CORN COOKIES
5.) PECAN PLUM CAKE
6.) BLACKBERRY PIE FILLING
7.) CORN PECAN COOKIES
8.) BLACKSTRAW CHEWIES
9.) SWEET OATMEAL BITES
10.) LITTLE FRUIT OR BERRY PIES
11.) MAPLE PECAN CANDY
12.) PECAN FRUIT CHEWIES
13.) CORN NUT SWEET PUDDING
14.) DELUXE 2-FOR-1 BAKED PUMPKIN

1.) CARROT CAKE MUFFINS

Uncle Joe called these "Bread-Cakes." They look like muffins, and are made in a regular muffin pan, but they are heavier and more moist (and sweeter) than regular dry muffins, more like cake. You could make them in a cake pan, but this is the way we have always made them, as individual cakes. He used rolled oats, but you can simply use uncooked old-fashioned oatmeal. You want only the very thin outermost skin of the orange. The whiter, inner part is bitter. Grate it with a fine-hole grater; this is called 'zest.' DON'T substitute milk for the buttermilk. Remember, 'spoon' means teaspoon.

Uncle Joe's recipe:

1 cup (unbleached) flour
1 half cup whole oats (use oatmeal)
1 half cup cornmeal
Handful pecans (just the meat – enough to make ½ cup chopped)
3 big eggs
Handful carrots (enough to make 1 cup chopped)
1 half cup raisins
1 cup buttermilk
1 quarter cup syrup (pure maple syrup with no extra sugar)
1 (tea)spoon bake powder
1 (tea)spoon bake soda
1 (tea)spoon salt
1 (tea)spoon cinnamon (powder)
1 (tea)spoon orange peel fine (fine grated colored skin - see note)
2 table spoons light oil (nut, seed or corn oil)
Bread-cake pan (he means a muffin pan)

Heat oven good. (Uncle Joe used a brick oven. Once again, I don't know how he knew how hot to get it. Set your modern oven for about 375 degrees or so.) Chop up pecans. Warm up syrup to pour. Beat up eggs. Put buttermilk, eggs and oil in big bowl. Mix up good. (He used a hand-whisk – if you use a mixer, use lower speed.) Put in oats, cornmeal, flour, bake powder, bake soda, cinnamon and salt. Mix but not too much. (If you beat too hard the batter will be tough.) Put in raisins, pecans, carrots, syrup and orange peel. Stir up good (blend thoroughly.) Butter pan good (grease with butter. He probably didn't have such a thing as store-bought liner papers. You can use those if you want to be able to handle the cakes later, but if you're just going to put them on the plate hot then grease the pan instead.) Bake light brown. (We would say golden-brown.) Makes one whole pan.

2.) BUTTER PECAN COOKIES

Good sweet plain old cookies, not fancy. Others nuts will work but pecans are best. Besides, we have them growing in the yard.

Uncle Joe's recipe:

1 half cup (unbleached) flour
1 half stick (unsalted) butter
1 half cup syrup (pure maple syrup – no extra sugar added!)
Little handful pecans (you will grind these – you only need enough ground meat to make a couple tablespoonfuls)
1 quarter (tea)spoon (ground) cinnamon
Big pinch salt

Heat up oven already medium hot. (He didn't use a thermometer. Set at baking heat, about 350 degrees.) Chop up pecans fine. Run through mill. (He had a grinder that he used for everything from grain to sausage. You can use a food processor. Essentially you're making coarse pecan meal, but it won't be dry – sort of pecan butter.) Sift flour fine. Put butter and syrup in pot on fire. Heat up good with bubbles (light boil.) Keep stirred! (It will burn if you don't. Heat just a minute. He used another term Mama couldn't remember, but it meant about a minute.) Take off fire. Put in flour, pecan, cinnamon and salt. Stir up real good. (Blend ingredients thoroughly. It should be nice and creamy.) Butter on pan. (Grease a cookie sheet with butter or light oil.) Big spoons of batter on pan. Put in oven. Make edges (golden-)brown and crispy. Eat hot. (Yep – they'll be gone before they have a chance to get cold. This is a good place to use some of that berry or pumpkin butter, but you will usually wind up eating them so fast -- as they come off the pan -- that you don't get around to buttering them.)

3.) STRAWBERRY CAKE

Good strawberries are hard to find at the store. If you know someone who grows them get those, otherwise just keep checking them at the store. Usually, the darker they are the sweeter. Get them as ripe as you can. Uncle Joe would often substitute fine corn meal for a portion of flour in his recipes. This makes the food richer and sweeter. Something that was a great treat in his time was to use real vanilla oil. That is expensive, compared to imitation vanilla, but well worth it. It will come in a tiny bottle, but you don't need as much of it as if you use the fake stuff. Uncle Joe called it flower-milk.

Uncle Joe's recipe:

2 (tea)spoons bake powder
2 cups (unbleached) flour
1 half cup cornmeal
1 cup syrup (pure maple syrup – no sugar added!)
Double handful strawberries (slice to make about 2 cups)
1 stick (unsalted) butter
4 big eggs
1 (tea)spoon flower-milk (vanilla oil)
Pinch cinnamon (powder)
(He called for a pinch of something else, too, that we think was ground cloves, and that's what we use)

Already heat up oven medium. (How did he know, with no thermometer? Set for 350 degrees.) Slice up strawberries little slices. Sift cornmeal fine. Warm up syrup to pour. Warm up butter to mix. Put syrup and butter in big bowl. Mix up good. (He used a hand whisk. Use your mixer on lower speed.) Beat up eggs. Put in eggs and (vanilla.) Mix up good. (Make light and creamy.) Put in bake powder, corn meal, flour, cinnamon and (cloves.) Mix up good. (Make sure all ingredients are thoroughly blended.) Butter (to grease) pan (it will take a regular 10 x 12 cake pan.) Put batter in. Put in strawberry slices. (Spread evenly across the batter.) Put in oven. Bake light-brown. (We would call it golden-brown.) Check with knife. (You want the knife to come out clean.) Cool little bit. Good with cold cream. (He means dairy cream, not makeup. I like it with vanilla ice cream.)

4.) LEMON CORN COOKIES

These are light cookies that look sort of like sugar cookies, but don't taste like cookie-shaped pieces of pure sugar. The lemon you use is the very thin outermost skin, fine-grated (sometimes called 'zest.') Don't get any of the whiter, inner peel; that part is bitter. You can use a fine-hole grater to make it, then use it while it's fresh. And here's another place to use real vanilla extract, not imitation. Uncle Joe called it flower-milk.

Uncle Joe's recipe:

1 (tea)spoon bake powder
1 half cup cornmeal
1 cup (unbleached) flour
1 half cup syrup (pure maple syrup with no sugar added)
1 stick (unsalted) butter
1 big egg
1 (tea)spoon lemon peel fine (fine-grated outer colored skin – see note)
1 (tea)spoon cinnamon (powder)
1 (tea)spoon flower-milk (vanilla extract)
Big pinch salt

Heat up oven already medium. (He didn't use a thermometer. Set yours to 350 degrees for baking.) Warm up syrup to pour. Warm up butter. Put syrup and butter in bowl. Mix up good. (Blend and make creamy.) Beat egg good. Put in egg and flower-milk (vanilla.) Mix up good (blend.) Put in bake powder, flour, cornmeal, lemon, salt and cinnamon. Mix up good. (He mixed by hand with spoons and a whisk.) Put in cool (refrigerator) to firm. Butter (to grease) pan (cookie sheet.) Put batter in cookie shapes with spoon. Put in oven, not long. (These are light cookies that won't take long to bake, about 10 minutes. They'll be sort of a crispy-gold looking.) Good warm. (They'll be a bit softer when they're still warm – very tasty.)

5.) PECAN PLUM CAKE

This is a heavy, rich sweet bread-cake sort of like banana-nut cake. Fresh from the oven it is really, really, really good. Uncle Joe used wild plums. If you get them at the store, usually the darker they are the sweeter. Get them right before you are going to cook them so you can get the ripest ones. Or, instead of plums you can use peaches, but it's hard to find store-bought peaches that have any flavor so if you use store-bought get nectarines instead. An important step is to boil the raisins first, but you don't boil them over the fire, just cover them with boiling water and let them soak. This softens them up. The orange peel is the very thin outermost skin, fine-grated (sometimes called 'zest.') Don't get any of the whiter, inner peel; that is bitter. Use a fine-hole grater to make it, then use it while it's fresh. Also, here again is the mystery ingredient that we're pretty sure was cloves. Whether he grew it or got it at the general store we don't know.

Uncle Joe's recipe:

3 (tea)spoons bake soda
4 cups (unbleached) flour
Big handful pecans (chop enough pecan meats to make 1 cup)
Double handful plums (about a pound worth after they're pitted)
1 cup raisins
1 stick (unsalted) butter
1 cup (pure) maple syrup (if the plums are sour or tart use 1 and a half cups)
1 (tea)spoon cinnamon (powder)
1 (tea)spoon salt
1 (tea)spoon orange peel fine (fine-grated outer colored skin – see note)
1 teaspoon (ground cloves)

Already heat up oven medium. (Set it for baking heat – 350 degrees.) Toast pecans (just the meat, not the shells.) Boil raisins. (Remember, don't boil them over the fire, just cover them with boiling water. Don't put too much, just enough to cover them. Let them soak for about half an hour so they'll get soft and plump.) Chop up pecans middle size pieces. Warm up butter to mix. Warm up syrup to pour. Mash up plums in big bowl with no pits. Put in syrup, butter and orange peel. Stir up good. Put in flour, bake soda, cinnamon, (cloves) and salt. Mix up good. (Blend all ingredients together thoroughly.) Put in raisins and pecans. Stir up good. (Mix the raisins and the pecan chunks through the batter evenly.) Butter (to grease) pan (cake pan.) Put batter. Bake. Check with knife. (You want the knife to come out clean. Should take about half an hour.) Cool. (Soon as it's not too hot to eat, then you eat it. This is a good place for fresh cold butter on top, or you can use the sweet pumpkin butter from the earlier recipe.)

6.) BLACKBERRY PIE FILLING

This is as good as it sounds. Blackberries are one of the sweetest berries I know of. You can use raspberries or blueberries, too. For that matter, you could use peaches, plums or strawberries. We always use blackberries because 1.) We like them best and 2.) They grow outside the house. Uncle Joe called for a cup and a half of maple syrup – that's what he liked. We use 1 cup of honey and a half cup of syrup. That is smoother. The orange you use is the very thin outermost skin, fine-grated (sometimes called 'zest.') Don't get any of the whiter, inner peel; that part is bitter. You can use a fine-hole grater to make it, then use it while it's fresh. If you use a store-bought pie-crust get one that doesn't have a bunch of sugar added to the pastry. That defeats the wonderful taste of the natural sweet ingredients. This is for one pie's worth.

Uncle Joe's recipe:

3 cups fresh blackberries
1 cup raisins
1 and half cups syrup (use 1 cup honey and 1 half cup pure maple syrup)
3 tablespoons orange peel fine (fine-grated outer colored skin – see note)
1 quarter stick (unsalted) butter
Handful (about 2 tablespoons) cornmeal
1 half (tea)spoon cinnamon (powder)
Big pinch salt

Have oven already hot for crust. (Set to bake at 400 degrees.) Boil water (in a separate pot. It won't take much.) Put berries, raisins, syrup (and honey,) orange peel (zest,) cornmeal, cinnamon and salt in pot (sauce pan.) Put in little bit boiling water (about half a cup. Just enough to help keep the mixture from burning.) Mix up. Put pot on medium fire. Make little boil (slow boil.) Keep stirred! (It will burn if you don't!) When boils make low fire. Cover up. Slow cook (simmer) little bit (about 5 minutes.) Warm up butter to mix. Put in pot and mix (stir the butter in and blend well.) Take off fire. Little bit cool ready to put in pie (have your pie crust ready.)

7.) CORN PECAN COOKIES

Good, crispy pecan treats. I've mentioned that Uncle Joe often substituted cornmeal for a portion of the flour. That works well here. Also, eggs make the batter nice and rich. You can use other nuts, but we like pecans best and they grow right by the house.

Uncle Joe's recipe:

Double handful pecans (coarsely chop enough for 1 cup)
1 cup cornmeal
1 half cup (unbleached) flour
1 half cup syrup (pure maple syrup with no extra sugar added)
2 big eggs
2 sticks (unsalted) butter
1 quarter (tea)spoon cinnamon (powder)
Pinch salt

Already heat up oven medium. (We've told how he didn't use a thermometer on his old wood-fired brick oven. Set yours for medium baking heat, 325 to 350 degrees.) Chop up pecans (the meat) little bits. Warm up butter and syrup to mix. Put in bowl. Mix with beater. (He used a heavy, old-time hand-whisk. Blend with your mixer until creamy.) Put in eggs (not the shells, of course; break them into the bowl.) Mix up good. Other bowl put flour, cornmeal, cinnamon and salt. Mix up good (blend thoroughly.) Put powders (dry mix) in big bowl with butter, syrup and eggs. Put in pecans (coarse-chopped pieces.) Stir up good (mixer on low here – you don't want to pulp the pecans.) Butter (to grease) big pan (cookie sheet. It will take a big one.) Put batter in cookie sizes with big spoon. Bake. Make light brown. (We would call it golden brown. When the edges get brown where they're thinner, that is just right.) Eat warm. (Good with cold milk.)

8.) BLACKSTRAW CHEWIES

These cookies have blackberries and strawberries in them. 'Blackstraw' was Daddy's name – nobody is sure what Uncle Joe called them. Pecans are the best kind of nut, although you can use walnuts if you don't have pecan trees in your yard like we do. Obviously, you should use fresh berries, not frozen.

Uncle Joe's recipe:

1 (tea)spoon bake soda
1 cup (unbleached) flour
1 cup cornmeal
Double handful (fresh) blackberries (cut in small pieces to make 1 cup)
Double handful (fresh) strawberries (same – 1 cup of cut small)
Handful pecans (chop the meat to make 1 half cup)
1 half cup syrup (pure maple syrup with no extra sugar)
1 big egg
1 stick (unsalted) butter
1 (tea)spoon cinnamon (powder)
Big pinch salt

Heat up oven already medium. (If you're not using a brick oven without a thermometer like Uncle Joe's, you can set your modern oven for regular baking heat – 350 degrees.) Chop up pecans. Cut up berries little pieces. Put cornmeal, flour, bake soda, cinnamon and salt in big bowl. Mix up good (blend thoroughly.) Warm up butter and syrup to mix. Other bowl beat up egg. Put in syrup and butter. Mix up good. (He used a hand-whisk. Use your mixer and make creamy.) Put in big bowl with dry mix. Mix up good (blend thoroughly.) Put in berries and pecans. Stir up good. (Hand stir to blend.) Butter (to grease) pan (big cookie sheet.) Put batter with spoon. Put in oven. Bake light. (Watch for the cookies to get a light, golden brown at the edges. This will be about 15 minutes.) Cool little bit. (When they're cool enough to handle, they're cool enough to eat.)

9.) SWEET OATMEAL BITES

Who doesn't like oatmeal cookies. These are regular old good ones. The recipe calls for oats; he meant rolled oats. Uncooked oatmeal will essentially give you the same effect. DO NOT use pre-cooked instant oatmeal – it will get tough and gummy. He highly prized vanilla oil. He called it 'flower-milk.' Real is much better than imitation. It costs a lot more but you use less, and it is worth the effort. You can use walnuts or something if you can't get pecans, but pecans are best.

Uncle Joe's recipe:

1 and half cups oats (old-fashioned uncooked oatmeal)
1 and half cups (unbleached) flour
Handful pecans (the meat chopped fine to make 1 half cup)
1 cup syrup (pure maple syrup with no sugar added)
2 sticks (unsalted) butter
1 (tea)spoon flower-milk (vanilla extract -- start conservative; use a half teaspoon)
Big pinch salt

Already heat up oven medium. (This is baking heat. Don't set any higher than 350 degrees – you don't want to make the oats tough.) Chop up pecans (the meat) fine pieces. Warm up butter and syrup to mix. Put butter and syrup in big bowl. Mix up good. (He used a hand whisk. Use your mixer and make creamy.) Put in flower-milk (vanilla oil.) Mix in. Put in oats, flour, pecans and salt. Mix up good. (Blend everything thoroughly.) Butter (to grease) big pan (cookie sheet.) Put batter cookie sizes with spoon. Put in oven. Make light brown. (We would call it golden-brown. When they get golden-brown around the edges, about 15 minutes, they are ready.) Cool little bit. (Don't wait too long, though, or somebody else will get them.)

10.) LITTLE FRUIT OR BERRY PIES

Long before anybody heard of pop-tarts these were around. You can use any fruit you like. Blackberries and muscadine grapes are sweetest. Strawberries, blueberries, peaches, plums, raspberries, all work good. Uncle Joe always just said 'berries,' since he used whatever was handy, so we left it that way. Use whichever kind you like. Also good to mix and match.

You can use any kind of pie pastry you like. The second part of the recipe is the pie shells, the way he made them.

Uncle Joe's recipe(s):

(The Filling:)
1 and half cup berries (or fruit - cut in small pieces.)
1 little sweet apple (cut up small to make a half cup)
1 half cup syrup (pure maple syrup with no extra sugar)
1 quarter (tea)spoon cinnamon (powder)
Cider (apple cider to moisten the mix to simmer. We usually just use apple juice.)

Cut up berries little pieces. Cut up sweet apples little bitty pieces. Warm up syrup to mix. Put berries, apple, syrup and cinnamon in little pan (sauce pan.) Put on medium fire. Little bit cider. (You need to add enough juice for the ingredients to simmer.) Get hot (not boiling but close.) Low fire (turn way down.) Slow cook (simmer, about 5 minutes.) Keep stirred (so it won't burn.) Take off fire (set aside while you prepare the pastry.)

For the pie shells:

1 (tea)spoon bake powder
1 and half cups (unbleached) flour
1 half stick (unsalted) butter
1 big egg
1 tablespoon syrup (pure maple syrup)
1 half (tea)spoon cinnamon (powder)
Little milk (to moisten the dough for rolling)
Big pinch salt

Already heat up oven hot. (He used a wood-fired brick oven, with no thermometer. Set yours for 375 degrees.) Warm up butter and syrup to mix. Beat up egg. Put bake powder, flour, cinnamon and salt in big bowl. Mix up good. Put in butter, syrup and egg. Mix good. (He used a hand-whisk. Use your mixer to blend all ingredients thoroughly.) Little bit milk. (You may need to add a little milk if the dough is too dry.) Roll out dough (on a flour-dusted pan or cabinet.) Make thin (like a pie crust.) Cut pie circles. (Cut 4 inch circles in the dough.) Big spoon berry filling on dough circle. Fold over and mash together. (Fold the dough over the filling and crimp the edges together. This gives you half-circle pies.) Poke holes (with fork, to vent for baking.) Butter pan (big cookie sheet.) Put pies (on pan.) Put in oven. Bake light brown. (We would say golden-brown. About 15 minutes.) Cool little bit. Put syrup on top. (Drizzle a little maple syrup on the tops of the pies while they're still warm. Start eating.)

11.) MAPLE PECAN CANDY

This is some serious candy. It is sort of like nut-brittle, but chewy instead of brittle. You will need a candy thermometer unless you have a lot of experience making candy. Although you can use any kind of nuts, you already know that we like pecans, and that we have them growing in the yard, so that's what's in the recipe. Use unsalted butter, and don't substitute milk for the cream. Uncle Joe used only maple syrup, but we like to substitute honey for some if it; this makes the overall effect smoother. He liked to make candy syrup, which he called 'sweet sauce.'

Uncle Joe's recipe:

Double handful pecans (You need enough chopped pecan meats to make 1 cup.)
3 cups syrup (use 1 cup pure maple syrup and 2 cups light honey)
1 half cup (whole) cream
1 tablespoon (unsalted) butter

Already toast pecans (just the meat. Not too long or they'll get tough.) Chop up in pieces. (Chop each half into four pieces. You need 1 cup of this.) Warm up syrup (and honey) to mix. (Stir the warmed honey and syrup to blend together.) Put in pot (saucepan) on medium fire. Put in cream. Keep stirred. Make sweet sauce. (His name for candy syrup. Here's where you need the candy thermometer. Bring the temperature of the 'sauce' up to 245 degrees. Keep stirred!) Put in butter. Stir good. (Blend the melted butter into the sauce.) Take off fire. Put in (toasted) pecans. Mix up good. (Stir until pecans meats are blended into the sauce well.) Butter (to grease) pan. Spread batter on. Let cool to firm. Make bites. (Cut into bite-sized squares. Eat this with cold milk or vanilla ice cream.)

12.) PECAN FRUIT CHEWIES

These are sort of like brownies, with fruit instead of chocolate. Here again you can use any kind of fruit, but Uncle Joe used peaches or plums. Peaches at the store don't have much taste nowadays. If you don't have home-grown peaches, then get nectarines at the store – you'll have a better shot at some taste. Store-bought plums usually are more promising. Get the darkest ones you can find; the more purple the sweeter, usually. Pecans are the best tasting nuts (and we have them in the yard) but you can use walnuts, too. Use maple syrup that doesn't have extra sugar added. Buttermilk is good in this; don't use sweet milk. Uncle Joe got real vanilla oil somewhere, which is expensive, but much better than the imitation and doesn't take as much. He called it 'flower-milk.'

Uncle Joe's recipe:

2 cups (unbleached) flour
Double handful peaches or plums (or whatever you like; berries will work, too. Cut up enough to make a cup and a half to two cups of small pieces.)
Double handful pecans (enough to make 1 cup of chopped nut meat)
2 big eggs (we always use jumbo size, and brown ones if you can find them. We used to keep laying hens but store eggs are fine)
1 cup syrup (pure maple syrup with no sugar added to it)
1 half cup buttermilk (NOT whole milk)
1 (tea)spoon (vanilla oil – OR LESS -- this much will make it pretty vanilla-y; start with half a teaspoon)
1 quarter (tea)spoon cinnamon (powder)
Cider (for cooking the fruit – apple juice will work)
Big pinch salt

Already heat up oven. (We've told how he used a wood-fired brick oven with no thermometer. Set your oven for low to medium baking; 325 degrees is good.) Cut up peaches or plums little pieces. Put in pot (saucepan) with cider (apple juice) to cook on medium fire. (Enough juice to cook the fruit in. Make it soft but not mushy. Keep it stirred so it won't burn.) Chop up pecans little pieces (just the meat, of course.) Beat up eggs. Warm up syrup to pour. Put eggs, buttermilk, syrup and flower-milk (vanilla) in big bowl. Mix up good. (He used an old-fashioned hand-whisk. Just use your mixer. Mix thoroughly until well-blended and creamy.) Put in flour, cinnamon and salt. Mix up good (until well-blended.) Put in (already cooked) fruit and pecans. Mix up good. Butter big pan (a regular old 10 by 12 inch is good. Butter works good as anything to grease.) Put batter (in pan.) Put in oven. Bake light brown. (We would say golden brown – not too dark! These will burn or get tough if you bake them too hard. 30 minutes should do it – keep checking.) Let cool. (If you try to cut them while they're hot they'll stick to the knife.) Little syrup on top. (He liked them sweet-sweet but I think they're plenty sweet without sweet-topping.)

13.) CORN NUT SWEET PUDDING

This is stiff, sort of like cheesecake filling. You use cornmeal instead of flour. Be sure the maple syrup is not the kind with extra sugar added. Although Uncle Joe used buttermilk in this recipe, we have always used sweet (whole) milk and that's what we recommend. Once again, pecans are about the best nut. And, you probably have begun to see that he liked cinnamon. We agree with him.

Uncle Joe's recipe:

1 quarter cup cornmeal
Double handful pecans (enough to chop up the meat pretty fine and make a cup and a half)
2 cups (whole) milk
3 big eggs
1 quarter stick (unsalted) butter (1 oz)
2 tablespoons syrup (pure maple syrup)
1 quarter (tea)spoon cinnamon (powder)
Big pinch salt

Already heat up oven. (He could set his wood-burning brick oven without a thermometer. Set yours for medium bake: 350 degrees.) Sift cornmeal fine. Chop up pecans fine. Warm up syrup to pour. Melt butter to mix. Put milk in pan over medium fire. Heat up good. (Don't boil.) Put in syrup and butter. Stir up good. (Get the syrup and melted butter blended well with the milk.) Put in cornmeal, pecans, cinnamon and salt. Stir up good. Don't cook too hot. (The mixture will burn if the heat is too high.) Keep stirring. (It will also burn if it's not kept stirred.) Make thick. (If the heat is right it will get well-thickened in about 15 minutes.) Take off fire. (Be sure it cools some before you put in the eggs! You don't want them cooked yet – they won't blend!) Beat up eggs good. Put in batter. Mix up good. (He had an old-fashioned hand-whisk. A modern mixer is even better.) Butter (to grease) pan. (This is a medium sized shallow cake pan or dish. He used iron and earthenware. We still have our ironware; you can use glass.) Pour everything (batter) in pan (dish.) Put in oven. Bake good. (30 minutes or so, not more than 45. You don't want the edges to get hard.) Scoop in bowls. (You can cut it into chunks.) Put cream and berries on top. (Absolutely.)

AND FINALLY:

14.) DELUXE 2-FOR-1 BAKED PUMPKIN

Our grand finale is a double-header dessert that gives you two for the price of one. If you've ever had pumpkin pie, you know pumpkin tastes pretty good. Pumpkins are naturally sweet. This is a way to cook the whole pumpkin and make a dandy desert that actually gives you two parts to eat. The stuffing serves as a marinade while cooking, then can be eaten by itself. Get the darkest, sweetest apples you can find. Toasting the pecans and cornmeal will bring out more flavor. And, here we'll find the mystery ingredient that everyone thinks must have been cloves, wherever he might have gotten those.

Uncle Joe's recipe:

1 little pumpkin (about 5 pounds – not a big one)
2 big sweet apples
1 cup raisins
Handful pecans (enough to make a half cup when chopped)
1 half cup cornmeal
1 half cup syrup (pure maple syrup with no sugar added)
1 (tea)spoon cinnamon (powder)
1 half (tea)spoon (cloves – at least that's what we use now)
Sweet cider (<u>sweet</u> apple cider – NOT cider vinegar – you can use apple juice)

Already heat oven medium. (Baking heat – 350 degrees. He didn't have a thermometer but he could get it just right in his wood-burning oven.) Chop up pecans (just the meat) little bitty pieces. Toast pecans (not too long or they'll get tough) and cornmeal. Soak raisins (cover with boiling water; soak 30 minutes to soften.) Cut up apples little pieces. Warm up syrup to pour. Put pecans, apples, raisins, cornmeal, syrup, cinnamon and (cloves) in pot. Put cider (enough to cover the ingredients so they will simmer and not burn.) Medium fire. Mix up good. Low fire (turn down.) Slow cook (simmer) little bit (5 minutes or so.) Keep stirred. (You don't want it to burn.) Take off fire and keep (set aside.) Cut pumpkin top and keep. (Save the top – you will use the top for a lid while the pumpkin is steaming.) Scoop out middle (seeds and pulp. Save the seeds to roast.) Poke holes in middle. (You need to poke plenty of holes in the inner surface of the pumpkin with a fork so that the stuffing will marinate into the pumpkin meat.) Put pumpkin in big pan. Pour in cider (around the pumpkin. It will be sitting in a baking dish with a couple inches of juice around it. We're going to steam the pumpkin.) Put sauce (the apple-raisin-pecan-syrup mixture) in pumpkin. Fill up with cider. (Fill the space on top of the stuffing with the juice.) Put top (the cut top of the pumpkin back on.) Put in oven. Bake. (In about 45 minutes the pumpkin will get soft enough that you can easily poke the outer skin with a fork.) Not too long! (If you over-cook the pumpkin it will shrivel and get tough.) Take out. (Here's our double-decker desert: Scoop out the fruit filling and put it on biscuits with cream over it. And, slice up the steamed, marinated pumpkin to eat like watermelon.)

And then:

ENJOY!

More from Rod Crossfield

SELECTED ADVENTURES
OF DETECTIVE DONNELLY

Rod Crossfield draws on his background in law enforcement to create this series of mysteries, in which Detective Lieutenant Joe Donnelly and Sergeant Brock are members of the under-staffed and over-worked homicide division of a big-city police department. The plodding, world-weary Donnelly and the cynical and irreverent Brock sift through a myriad of misleading clues and conflicting statements to identify the murderers.

More from Rod Crossfield

**REMEMBERING THE GOOD STUFF:
MEMOIRS FROM THE HEARTLAND**

Rod has worked across the country and around the world. He has enjoyed careers as a commercial pilot, a policeman, a construction engineer, a long-haul truck driver, a teacher and a television producer. He writes with wit and witticism of the humorous characters he has encountered in his travels and provides fascinating insight into the nuts and bolts of some of the occupations that have earned his living.

More from Rod Crossfield

Rod Crossfield writes a series of articles that tell the way the world is and the way it should be. He describes real people in real life and he places accountability squarely on those who seek to avoid it.

Whether he arouses acknowledgment or denial his observations and analyses will strike home.

Read his commentary at itsayshere.com

rodcrossfield.com

WESTFIELD MEDIA
WM

LaVergne, TN USA
01 September 2009
156665LV00001B/53/P

9 781607 254447